D1391519

Skipper and Mate in "Senorita's" cockpit

"SENORITA"

BY

HENRY REYNOLDS

Author of *Coastwise—Cross-Seas,*
Spanish Waters, etc.

WITH A PREFACE BY

. H. J. HANSON, O.B.E.

AND

ILLUSTRATIONS FROM PHOTOGRAPHS

LONDON
PETER DAVIES

First Published in 1936

MADE AND PRINTED FOR PETER DAVIES LTD. BY
MORRISON AND GIBB LTD., LONDON AND EDINBURGH

CONTENTS

v

LIST OF ILLUSTRATIONS

"SENORITA"

Tonnage, reg.   5·91
    ,,   Thames, 7

LBP	29 ft. 0 in.
Breadth	8 ft. 0 in.
Depth	5 ft. 3 in.

Built by BARR, Wivenhoe, 1879

> *"Nunc vino pellite curas:*
> *Cras ingens iterabimus aequor."*

"Quaff your Reynolds in the Winter and go forth to sea in the Spring."

CHILDERS and Reynolds hold the lead as descriptive writers of cruising tales, so says the Oracle; and those of Henry Reynolds describe actual voyages in the waters which extend from Norway and Shetland to Spain.

Reynolds was a hard case, his ships small craft of about 30 feet in length, and if the general reader can realize that his discomforts at sea arose from a scanty supply of cash, *res angusta domi* as he was fond of quoting, and from leisure insufficient for his ambitious programme; and that such persistent ill-fortune as he describes does not, at all times, pursue the sailorman; she and he will find this volume full of fascination.

Reynolds would cast himself upon the waters at a long pre-arranged date, with an ambitious non-stop objective, maybe hundreds of miles to windward, blow high, blow low. But he would never renew the laces in his boots, not until they parted!

not run two nov...
stop, then three days ho... to ...y, ...
prostrate novices!

Yet let not the young seaman of to-day take
alarm at his eternal struggles with the elements
and his ship's gear, for it was in 1880 that
Reynolds bought *Elaine*, 1885 that he com-
missioned *Senorita*, born of Barr of Wivenhoe in
'77, and 1895 saw the birth of *Winnie*; and what
though the climate may be the same, the young
seaman has the advantage now of an easier ship,
lighter and stronger gear of improved design,
and of far greater facilities for keeping them in
order, so that with the help of his auxiliary engine,
he is able better to adjust the ambition of his
programme to whatever may be his degree of
nautical tenacity and peripateticity.

So let him read these yarns with diligence, and
he will find them full of charm and teeming with
incident and things seen, and methods sometimes
obviously best avoided, all which afford a sea-
going education in themselves.

And now for the purpose of these yarns:
Henry Reynolds began life in 1854, the parents
lived on the Deben at Woodbridge from 1866,
and the boy sailed small boats; he converted an
Aldeburgh 20-foot beach boat in 1880, bought
Senorita in 1885, and *Winnie* in 1911. He took
his degree at Cambridge, and turned to school-

mastering, not on account of its attraction, but because "needs must when the devil drives." He retired after the war, and he wrote sea tales to help the ship's husband. Those included in this volume he sold to the Cruising Association, and little by little since 1922 they have appeared privately in the *Cruising Association Bulletin*. Alas, he had the misfortune in 1925, one naughty August morning in the Sound of Jura, to lose his devoted *Winnie*. This passage is 15 miles long and 3 miles wide, 40 fathoms for the lead till within two cables of the shore, its continuous use most difficult in the conditions prevailing, the wind bitter, the darkness intense, a cataclysm of rain, and above Ardlussa a 4½-knot stream runs springs and neaps.

They sailed blind upon the rocks of Ardlussa, and were lucky to climb a slippery wall of rock to safety.

To the young seaman who seeks a way out of this situation, in the abstract, let him remember the three anchorages off Gigha, 22 miles short of Ardlussa; one of these twelve hours sooner or a run back early in the day are the alternatives to a difficult task which the elements proved to have in store for Reynolds.

Reynolds wrote truly when he said it mattered not how often the same expanse of water were covered, one might be quite sure that, on each occasion, circumstances and incidents would differ entirely from any that had been before experienced; the contrariety of the unexpected was not the least of the many charms of cruising, and for forty years he traversed parts of the same old road without a line that lacks interest.

As these various voyages run their natural course, he records many details which may be of great instructive value to the young seaman, often, it is true, warnings of what should be avoided.

He tells of the difficulties of the narrows of the Dartmouth entrance, off Kettle Point, a spot whose anxieties are possibly unknown to most of the auxiliary generation, but one where the pure sail craft may have a very anxious time, becalmed in a gale of wind awaiting a puff to carry her clear of the rocky point towards which she is drifting on the stream and heaving on the breathless swell.

He tells of passing the Bill of Portland under various conditions, of the South Ship entrance to the roadstead—called the *Hole in the Wall*—closed since the war by a block ship. Many may wonder why this ship has not been removed, for it blocks what was a useful entrance. One reason may be that since the obstruction of the stream through this entrance, the roll which used to set the big ships in rhythmic motion has not been felt by them. He tells of St. Alban's Race, of which experienced amateurs hold differing views; Reynolds never found it really angry, but it is and it sometimes leads to accident; an 18-foot bamboo, used also for sounding, and as aerial yard, helps safe transfer, for some Light Vessels are far from steady in the tideway, and if you are really close, a swerve, and a davit may catch, or a parrot perch may foul.

Continental *harbour basins* Reynolds preferred to view from outside; traffic, coal dust, and other matter may make them extremely uncomfortable, but there are seasons with some of them when you may find the fleet away, and they may then afford a very pleasant centre of operations to explore the neighbourhood, such as St. Malo, Paimpol, La Palais, St. Martin, and La Rochelle, at the proper time.

His *topsail sheet* did not fail to perform that conjuring trick of hitching itself around the peak, and the young seaman may be able to forestall this hitch if he makes a mental note to moderate the amount of slack. On *night sailing*: he thinks many amateurs miss a great delight in showing repugnance to the dark hours at sea. On *anchoring*: he holds it is better to be sure than sorry and always laid a kedge. On *ancient pumps* he spent many weary hours, and welcomed the introduction of the semi-rotary, while to-day he would welcome the diaphragm pump, which leaves the other dry—it may want new diaphragms, and without a supply it is useless. We are told it has the digestion of an ostrich.

On *laying up* Reynolds gives the yacht yards
good marks, in his experience, though he had a
misfire at Dunlaoghaire. I recall a similar experience on the opposite side of the Emerald
Island, at Cahersiveen, where the local infants
laid out the mainsail on the quay as it was too
muddy for marbles and other games.

On the *ancient lamps* of the 'eighties he has somewhat to say; he had much trouble with his colza
wicks, difficult to light and to keep alight—
camphor helps matters. Then he tried Cera, this
is just a candle wax burnt in a copper container
with a copper wire standing therein, and having
a curl over the top of the flame which keeps the
wax liquid; extinguish it, and the wax sets, and
no mess.

We took one of these across the German
frontier at Emmerick when cruising up the
Rhine, and a stout customs officer in very hot
weather, demurring to my statement that it was a
wax for burning in a lamp, inquired, "Was ist
denn das?" "Wachs, Wachs zum brennen!"
"Nay, nay, das kann nicht sein!" He entered his
finger into our stock and ate a lump of it. I made
use of a somewhat familiar German expression,
"Stimmt?", but he seemed to enjoy its taste and
texture. Reynolds was keen on a good cockpit
light, he was once saved from collision by
burning a whole box of matches in one; and he
was an occasional victim of that queer sort of

up and down motion which gave him the notion he never was meant for the sea; he held it was a matter of pluck and endurance to overcome seasickness. Some people call it will, but will is powerless to command a refractory stomach.

He records being caught by the heel on a fishing-net at sea in the dark and no harm done; we once took the trouble in the dark to sail round a huge fleet of fishermen at work off White-sand Bay, and in the morning were told we could have sailed straight through without doing any harm.

On the subject of *keeping a good look out*, Reynolds tells an eloquent story of his helmsman, who had the wind free, and failed to see a big smack close-hauled, till she came about, to avoid a collision close under his lee; this had a moral: "Go 'ome to yar mother an' git 'er to tie ye fast to a cheer! Gawd's trooth, ye ain't fit to be let out alone wi'out a nuss."

On his Irish cruise Reynolds mentions passing Tara Hill—Tara, in Wexford, abreast the Arklow LV. This is not where "the harp shed the soul of music through Tara's halls," that was at Tara, Co. Meath, a sacred spot held to date from the Bronze Age, as the centre of government, and still the symbol of national unity. The harp is shown with the Book of Kells at Trinity, Dublin, but there is no birth certificate with it. There

2

are no halls at Tara, *pace* the shades of Moore, nor have been for fourteen centuries maybe.

Reynolds' sailing was confined to the Easter and August holiday periods, and writing after the the war, he speculates as to whether the Augusts of the early 'nineties were a special breed. I fancy many who were sailing then would have the same feeling—weather seems to run in cycles, long periods of settled summer weather were a matter of course in the 'nineties, according to my recollection.

When he opines that fair winds are not sent to be lightly wasted, let the young seaman take note and act thereon.

A foul wind always follows a fair one in these climes, so catch them while you may. He is emphatic on the inferiority of the gear and rigging of the 'eighties—clumsy rig, huge jibs with low foot, running topmasts with fid which usually failed to trip from the deck, long reefing bowsprits with a generous steeve, square-headed topsails and heavy canvas.

Referring again to the past, from the beach at Aldeburgh, Reynolds pictures the scene on a fine summer evening in 1868 after a long spell of S.W. winds, when a large fleet of sailing vessels of all sorts and sizes, some bound down under, and some to the river Thames, clippers, barques, colliers, and all sorts, passed before him with every stitch set.

Once again in 1893 he recalls a similar occasion.

Reynolds had no prejudice against engines in other vessels, but delighted, himself, to rely on sails and seamanship. Not infrequently his "hardy ruffian" appearance when, unkempt and in sea rig, he sought officials and stores ashore, involved him in little difficulties.

Two books from his pen were published during his lifetime, *Coastwise—Cross-Seas*, and *Spanish Waters*. Reynolds would play bridge, he enjoyed dancing greatly, and latterly derived consolation from his garden. Fear had no place in his constitution or vocabulary. He suffered a long and trying illness with great courage before his end in 1929.

Four lines from R. A. Hopwood's " The Old Way," a great favourite of his, form an appropriate epitaph:

"There's a wondrous Golden Harbour, far beyond the setting sun,
Where a gallant ship may anchor when her fighting days are done,
Free from tempest, swell, and battle, toil and tumult safely o'er,
Where the breezes murmur softly and there's peace for evermore."

I

DOWN CHANNEL

Oh, who can tell save he whose heart hath tried
And danced in triumph o'er the waters wide,
The exulting sense, the pulse's maddening play,
That thrills the wanderer of that trackless way?

BYRON.

WHEN one is absolutely debarred from the use of the sea, a certain amount of comfort is, undoubtedly, to be drawn from the perusal of one's ancient logs. Refreshed by the reading of hastily scribbled and half obliterated pages, the memory recalls with unexpected vividness the many whimseys of a capricious mistress; the weary days of pitching slowly to windward, when the white-capped seas, with remorseless persistence, sweep down upon the labouring ship; the days of exasperating calm, when the surface of the ocean gently heaves like the breast of a sleeping giant; the rarer days of bright sunshine and strong fair wind, when the mind almost fears that fate has some ill in store to counter-balance excess of happiness; the days of fog, of stress, of danger even, when a man is tempted to curse the sea and the folly that sent him forth to wander on its bosom; the days of triumph due to bold decision, or of punishment inflicted upon timid hesitation, for, while nothing can surpass the charm of the sea in its happier moods, nothing can be more dour than the sea in the exaction of vengeance for mistakes made or for opportunities lost.

In January 1885 I bought the *Senorita* of 6 tons registered burden. Of her it is sufficient here to say that she proved an exceptionally good boat, and for twenty-five years was the joy of a laborious life.

On 29th July we joined the yacht at Woodbridge, a crew of schoolmasters, four—well—schoolmasters. A reader of the baser sort will readily supply from his own vocabulary the epithet which, in our sense of irresponsibility, we did not hesitate to apply to ourselves. A brother who in later years fell away from grace and took to golf but was, as yet, as enthusiastic and as inexperienced a cruiser as his skipper, ably filled the post of chief mate. The other two were, respectively, a colleague of my own, who may be called the steward, and a friend of my brother whose mild look and gentle bearing won for him at once the incongruous title of the Pirate. The former came for only a few days to pass away the time till he joined two engaged upon an adventurous trip by river and canal across Europe to the Black Sea. The latter, considerably older and much more staid of demeanour, almost succeeded in imparting to a riotous crew an air of sober respectability. He was a genial man and an amusing companion, but utterly ignorant of the

sea and of life on a yacht; he was cursed with
timorous nerves and an unquenchable objection
to the smallest discomfort.

The yacht was bound down Channel. The
Wight had been already visited, and our hearts
were filled with a longing to extend our ex-
plorations farther westward. But, eager as we
were to start upon our venture, we delayed several
days in the river. The hamlet at the mouth of the
Deben was filled with a crowd of cousins and their
friends, all damsels, ranging in age from thirteen
to twenty. What chance had four unattached men
with a lot of girls only lightly chaperoned by an
easy-going aunt? The Pirate, certainly, was
married, but his insistence on the fact was
lamentably weak. Nay, he backed up with suspicious alacrity the protest of the girls that a short
delay to give them a few sails up the river and out
to sea could in no way be detrimental to the
success of the cruise. The flappers, with the bold-
ness of their age, openly declared an affection for
the skipper which would have been embarrassing
had he not fortunately been blessed with sense
enough to know that their affection was rather
for the *Senorita* than for himself. Their numbers
were large, and there is safety in numbers:

> "So we went strolling down by the rolling,
>   Down by the rolling sea.
>   If you can't be true to one or two,
>   You're much better off with three."

The morality of the lines may be questioned by the "unco guid," but it is a type of morality that has preserved many a young man from a too hasty plunge into the deep sea of matrimony.

It was not till 6th August that the crew was persuaded to lay aside dalliance and to make a belated start. The wind was light E. by N. As the yacht slowly pushed her way towards the bar against the last of the flood-tide, frequent glances were turned to blind-blocked windows, behind which lay sleeping many professedly disconsolate maidens. Not one peeped out to see us go, not a hand waved a tear-saturated handkerchief in token of farewell. Most of the crew wore an air of depression and showed considerable grumpiness of temper, but lowness of spirit and grumpiness may well have been due, not so much to disappointment, as to the dank chill of early morn. The Pirate in particular looked distinctly miserable.

"Faithless little Kitty!" he murmured, apostrophising his fourteen-year-old comrade of the last few days, "who was going to rise at daylight to cheer the sorrow of her departing swain!"

"Oh, rot!" quoth the steward as he carefully filled the lid-fitted bowl of a huge pipe. "Females are all alike, old or young, black or white—off with the old love, on with the new—out of sight, out of mind!" The steward was only twenty-five, but he spoke with the bitterness of a dyspeptic cynic of eighty.

At 6 a.m. the yacht crossed the bar. We held out boldly to sea, passed the Sunk lightship, weathered the Long Sand Head bell buoy and, though the weather was inclined to be thick, found without any great difficulty the Kentish Knock lightship. Various causes had always hitherto prevented us traversing this passage through the sands. With its athwart-running tides it is not entirely devoid of difficulty. Its tossing sand-laden waters showed grey against the gloomy atmosphere, and our range of vision was by no means widely extended. But when once the Kentish Knock lightship was found and passed, all anxiety was over. Our course thence to the N. Foreland was clear. The sense of success and the steady E. wind raised our spirits to a high pitch. In fond imagination we crossed unnumbered leagues of water in an incredibly short space of time. Youthful cruisers are shockingly prone to count too soon their unhatched chickens.

All day the yacht had an opposing tide to stem. By 4 p.m., when she passed the N. Foreland, the wind had fallen very light. Only slowly she dragged her lagging way down the Gull Stream. At 8 p.m. it was quite calm, and the E. running stream began to sweep her back. Fitful breezes off the land enabled her to regain some of the lost ground. At midnight, when steward and skipper went below, she was barely abreast of Deal. The Pirate turned out willingly, for he had not been at all happy in the cabin. He had resented the extinguishing of the lamp and the frustration of his plan of quieting his nerves through the hours of darkness by losing himself in the obscurities of an abstruse treatise on philosophy.

At 2 a.m., off the S. Foreland, the watch below was hurriedly roused to stow the topsail. A squall of wind and rain had suddenly struck the yacht. The *Senorita* in those days carried a long topmast on which was set a jib-headed topsail, held to the mast by a jack-stay, a convenient and fairly effective substitute for a lacing. For a moment the topsail refused to answer to our pulling. "Cut it! cut it!" yelled the Pirate, who had scrambled forward and was clinging for dear life to the weather rigging.

"Cut what?" we asked wrathfully as we threw our weight on the topsail tack.

"Cut it! cut anything!" was the excited reply, and had the Pirate had a knife on his person, there is little doubt that he would have slashed at the peak or jib halliards in his frantic desire to do something to relieve the ship. Fortunately we soon succeeded in overcoming the obstruction, and brought the sail to the deck. Whilst we changed our wet clothes, a heavy thunderstorm burst over the yacht. The Pirate evidently was no lover of lightning. As we tumbled off to sleep again, we could hear him in the cockpit detailing to the mate the gruesome horrors wrought within his knowledge by the misdirected energy of electric currents. A heavy thunderstorm at sea can be quite an awe-inspiring experience, and the Pirate may easily be forgiven for some display of nervousness.

Just before daylight we were compelled to reef down. The wind had come up strong from W.S.W. and the weather-running tide was increasing every moment the execrable sea which is usually to be found in the neighbourhood of Dover. For a couple of hours the yacht was worked to windward in the vain hope that a possible slant might enable her to reach the shelter of Dungeness. In the end, owing to further increase of wind and cessation of favouring tide, we were compelled to give up the struggle and to run back to Dover. At 6 a.m. the yacht was lying at the entrance of the dock waiting for the gates to be opened. As I leant on the boom aft, wet and cold and generally disgusted, the steward emerged from below with a bottle in his hand and a twinkle in his eye :

"Would you like a drop of rum, Skipper?"

Would I like a drop of rum! It was what I had been longing for without knowing it. As I took a good swig from the bottle, I learnt that it was a sample of a special brand, which the steward had purloined from the home cellar, and had carefully reserved for such circumstances as the present. The glow in our veins induced such

generosity that we foolishly handed up the bottle
to a lock-gate man whose eyes were bulging out
of his head with ungovernable desire. It was a
piece of singularly misplaced confidence. The
man threw back his head and literally poured
the spirit down his capacious throat. In our turn,
we showed bulging eyes of anxiety. Only with
difficulty was the bottle recovered.

"Proper stuff, that!" grunted the man.

"Dash it!" growled the steward as he ruefully
gauged with his eye the amount that had disappeared. "If that isn't the reward of kindness!
That's the sort of treatment that dries up the well
of generosity! Why, it is simply biting the hand
of a benefactor." More remarks couched in
similar strain, not addressed directly to the man,
but pointed at him and intended to hurt, quickly
roused his temper to fury. Gifted with little power
of banter, he betook himself to vulgar abuse,
reminding the Pirate, who had a fine knowledge
of Milton, of the lines in "Comus":

> "For swinish Gluttony
> Ne'er looks to heaven amidst his gorgeous feast,
> But with besotted base ingratitude
> Crams, and blasphemes his Feeder."

The weather set in thoroughly bad. The steward
left to join his friends on their transcontinental
trip. We scarcely met again till 1911 when he
joined us on the *Winnie* for the trip to Spain.
Dover struck us as a very dull place. In a few

days we were thoroughly weary of the dock and the town. Unable to advance westward, we ran under close reefed canvas to Ramsgate. There, though the place offered more distractions to idle men, we were compelled to eat out our hearts with vexation for several further days. The Pirate, tired apparently of the mild roughing which life on board entailed, suddenly decided to take his departure. Later, he repented of his hasty action and spent a small fortune in telegraphing to all likely ports on the S. coast, in the hope of getting in touch with us and joining the yacht again. But none of his telegrams came to our hands and his money was wasted.

In the very early hours of Friday, 14th August, we towed the yacht out of dock and lay to a buoy in the outer harbour. Tempted by a N.W. breeze, we slipped away at 3.30 a.m. The tide was still pouring eastward and, outside, the wind was very faint. We had only light wind all day, but by the evening the yacht was nearly down to Eastbourne. Not till 2 a.m. on the following morning was Beachy Head passed. Nothing of particular interest happened the following day. We were again troubled by light and varying breezes. At 5 p.m., with a N.E. draught and strong W.-running tide, the yacht passed the Mixon beacon and was soon through the Looe channel. At 10.30 p.m. we anchored between the Warner and Bembridge fort in a flat calm.

For a few days we cruised about the waters of the Wight, making Wootton creek our head-quarters. Our friend, Frank Cowper, had a house upon its W. bank. Whilst the creek provided quiet anchorage for the yacht, Cowper overwhelmed her crew with prodigal hospitality. We were only too glad to exchange the results of our rude cooking for the delicacies provided by a well-appointed kitchen. The least gluttonous are swayed by the promptings of appetite. The Israelites, in their longing for the flesh-pots of Egypt, were willing to condone the hardships of slavery.

On Wednesday, 19th August, at 6 a.m., with light wind about N., we wriggled out of the creek. The tide was pouring westward. At 9 a.m. the yacht was shot through the Needles passage. Rather a dreary day followed, of calms and paltry flaws. We were entering an entirely new world, but there was sufficient haze to obscure the sandy cliffs the yacht was drifting past. At 6 p.m. she was not far from Standfast point. A little N.W. breeze was sending her gaily over a calm sea and weather-going tide. Weak nature suggested a night in Swanage. The calm waters of its bay offered an almost irresistible temptation. But the temptation was sternly strangled. After a day of calm a breeze was not to be lightly wasted. Moreover, the mate had friends at Weymouth whom he wished to visit. Our time was insufficient to allow a visit to both places.

It was a beautiful night with a bright moon and a fine breeze. Before long there shone out ahead the Portland and Shambles lights. The yacht splashed through St. Alban's Race. In due time she was tacked towards the land. A period of calm, just at daylight, gave us ample opportunity to scan the cliffs that circle round the bay. The breeze came again, and at 7 a.m. we anchored off the end of Weymouth Pier, inside a fleet of racing yachts, already setting their canvas for the day's regatta. The mate found his friends. We gave them a sail; they gave us a supper.

At 6 a.m. we left Weymouth with a light N.N.W. wind and, running through Portland harbour, accomplished in safety the passage round the Bill. As Pope so wisely writes:

"Fools rush in where angels fear to tread."

What must especially annoy the angels is the fact that the fools, as often as not, come safely through the danger into which they have blindly rushed. Years later, we learnt the need of respectful attention to the tides in making this passage perilous. That we escaped the disaster of being swept into the race is a conclusive proof that Providence had us for the moment in its safe keeping. The contemplation of some of my earlier escapades nearly compels acquiescence in the verdict of various candid friends that, as drowning is obviously regarded as too honourable a death, destiny must hold hanging in reserve as my ultimate fate.

Till 11.30 a.m. the yacht was kept upon the starboard tack. On port tack she headed N.W. About 3 p.m. land was sighted broad on our lee beam. Some rain fell and was followed by a flat calm. The yacht was far from the land, but was found to be abreast of Sidmouth. At 5 p.m. a N. breeze began to send the yacht towards Torbay within the shelter of which we had determined to seek rest. But the breeze did not blow for long, and the ensuing calm lasted till nearly midnight.

A fine N.W. breeze piped up. The yacht, with topsail and big jib set, rattled away over the smooth water towards the Start, the light of which ahead seemed to beckon her onwards. The fine breeze and the beauty of the night easily persuaded us to forego the comfort of Torbay or of Dartmouth. Moreover, we were both yet a little averse from tackling strange harbours in the dark. The repugnance shown to night sailing by many lovers of the sea is a pitiable mistake. Little they realize what pleasure they are missing. My most delightful recollections are connected with night passages. The memory of this two hours' sail, while the yacht, in the moon's deceptive light, seemed to carry a very cloud of straining canvas and to rush through the water with the speed of the *Flying Dutchman*, will never fade from my mind, till all memories fade in the shadow of death.

The breeze carried us to the Start and then abruptly expired. The time was 2 a.m. Not till 6 a.m., when a W. draught came, were we able to draw away from the serrated edge of the Start's extremity. With a W. setting stream and a wind improving in quantity, the yacht worked quickly past Prawle point and the lofty granite cliffs that stretch from Bolt head to Bolt Tail. At 2 p.m. we had Plymouth breakwater ahead, and were hesitating about which entrance to use to make the harbour. We were by no means confident of the existence of an entrance at the E. end of the breakwater. Whilst we were still in doubt and vainly hoping that a passing vessel might solve our difficulty, the wind, which had been for some time growing softer, vanished with almost dramatic suddenness. The sun shone down upon us with blistering heat. Over the land the massing of a dense black cloud portended a thunderstorm. But the cloud worked slowly inland and our weather remained unchanged.

In those days there was no *Cruising Association Handbook* to help the inexperienced voyager in his choice of a berth in a strange harbour, and many years were yet to pass before the Admiralty Sailing Directions were brought to my notice. Consequently, when, at 6 p.m., the yacht influenced by the sweep and the faintest flutter from S. in her sails, at last crept slowly round the lighthouse at the W. end of the breakwater,

3

we had not the vaguest notion where to find a comfortable and convenient anchorage. We were in no way hustled; ample time was given for choice. Eventually we let the anchor go under the E. shore in Jenny Cliff bay. In our chart this portion of the Sound was labelled " Merchant's Anchorage," whence we concluded that our lying there would be no inconvenience to the naval authorities. That seemed to be the only redeeming feature of the chosen berth.

But still weather continued, and we spent a quiet night. In the morning our pull in the dinghy to Sutton Pool proved our distance from everywhere. We laid in some provisions, and were shaved at an unpretentious barber's shop. The barber was a stout old gentleman who, like Falstaff, larded the lean earth with the perspiration produced either by the warmth of the day or the energy of his exertions. After removing, with no great skill but punctilious thoroughness, the bristly growth of several days, he was unaffectedly amused by an affirmative reply to his perfunctory inquiry if any water were wanted. His usual clients, evidently, imagined that after a clean shave at his hands there was nothing left for a sponge and water to remove. We left the shop strangely conscious of our chins, but, as the worthy man charged us only a penny each for his labour, we felt that we had little ground for grumbling. To a painful operation there had not been added the imposition of an excessive charge.

Returning on board we weighed anchor. At 1 p.m. under all sail, with wind S., we passed Rame head and set our course W. by N. for Falmouth. Thick fog suddenly descended. A yawl unexpectedly appeared ahead. We passed each other in safety without, however, any too much room to spare. When the fog lifted at 7 p.m., we found ourselves abreast of Fowey but far out from the land. The wind came up from S.E. but fell very light, and the tide, too, must have been setting eastwards, for it was 11 p.m. when the yacht passed the Dodman. At midnight I turned out the mate and went below. When he roused me at 4 a.m. from a sound sleep, the yacht was laid to on the port tack with St. Anthony's light shining out astern. The wind was strong from E. and growing stronger every moment. The yacht had been lying to for some time. Entirely ignorant of Falmouth, we had decided before I left the deck to remain outside till daylight. The topsail was pulled down, and as there would be sufficient daylight by the time St. Anthony was reached to lighten our way, the yacht was headed straight for the harbour. The wind was beginning to blow spitefully and a heavy sea chased us as we fled under a great press of canvas to the inviting shelter of a comfortable haven.

Safety was gained but no comfort. A chart of the harbour was on board but could not be found at the moment. It was barely daylight as the yacht flew past the Black Rock, and St. Mawes creek escaped our notice; nor, in the general gloom, were the masts visible of the vessels lying off the town. The violence of the wind was now so great that to get canvas off the yacht was a matter of immediate necessity. The anchor was hastily let go in the Cross roads not far from the *Ganges*, a training ship which, some years later, was shifted to Harwich. We had chosen a berth exposed to every wind that blew, but we showed a certain method in the madness of our choice. The harbour was full of big sailing ships. Any fresh arrivals would assuredly leave a clear berth to the bulky *Ganges* and, thereby, would threaten neither danger nor disturbance to the little *Senorita*.

It proved to be, as we had anticipated, a most uncomfortable anchorage. The yacht pitched and rolled and ran about like a cat possessed of a devil. The next day, though it rained heavily and the E. wind blew almost with the force of a gale, wearied with the incessant motion and fearing lest a foul anchor might prove our undoing, we put the yacht under snug canvas and sailed away upon an exploring expedition. The easy motion of sailing comforted greatly bodies that ached in every joint from the jolting they had endured for more than twenty-four hours. We examined the anchorage under Falmouth Town and, after cruising about among the anchored ships, brought up late in the afternoon in St. Mawes creek, opposite the village. That night we slept well. The sound of wind in the trees and the lapping against the yacht's side of miniature billows scarcely disturbed the serenity of the tranquil haven into which we had penetrated.

The following morning the clanking of a vessel's windlass dragged me unwillingly from the blankets. A neighbouring ketch was weighing anchor. The time was 6 a.m. and the weather dull. A gentle S.W. wind was blowing. It was time for us to be making homeward, for the date was 27th August, and even a schoolmaster's holidays do not last for ever. We weighed the anchor and departed in complete ignorance of the beauties we were leaving behind unviewed. Many years passed before we discovered what is to be found:

"By St. Anthony's in Roseland where the fern and fuchsia grow."[1]

At 8 a.m. we rounded St. Anthony and squared away for the Dodman. Soon a dense fog settled over the sea. Somewhere off the Dodman a smack, working to windward, hailed us to know if the yacht was E. of the Head. We thought she was but could not speak with certainty. The wind gradually backed so far that the yacht could not

[1] "By St. Anthony in Roseland"—a fine poem published in *Punch*.

quite lay the course. She made the land eventually 2 miles W. of Rame head. The fog lifted, but the head wind and the threatening sky sent us without discussion into Plymouth Sound. At 7 p.m. we brought up near our former berth, and went to bed betimes in the not very confident hope that an early hour would see the yacht speeding upon her way eastwards.

During the night it blew hard at times, but when we looked out at 5.30 a.m., there did not appear to be any great weight in the wind. On the other hand, it was due E. and the sky wore a most unpromising look. Anxious as we were to hurry on, we hesitated to start and determined to have breakfast before we came to a decision. Before the kettle boiled, the wind blew up with great strength. This settled the matter. The stove was extinguished and a return made to bed. The comfort of the blankets was a slight compensation for our disappointment, and a late breakfast shortened the weary hours of waiting.

All day it blew hard with a bright sun and clear sky. There was no lack of movement in the Sound. Coaster after coaster rushed in and brought up in Jenny Cliff bay. We failed to sight at 1 p.m. the fall of the time-ball upon Mount Wyse and did not hear the signal gun. The only mention of Mount Wyse to be found in literature, so far as I know, is in a poem by Captain Marryat, bearing the title of "Port Admiral."

" 'Twas at the landing-place that's just below Mount Wyse,
  Poll leaned against the sentry's box, a tear in both her
    eyes;
Her apron twisted round her arms, all for to keep them
    warm,
Being a windy Christmas Day, and also a snowstorm—
      And Bet and Sue
      Both stood there too,
        A-shivering by her side;
      They both were dumb,
      And both looked glum,
        As they watched the ebbing tide.
      Poll put her arms a-kimbo,
        At the Admiral's house looked she,
      To thoughts before in limbo
        She now a vent gave free—
      You have sent the ship in a gale to work,
        On a lee shore to be jammed,
      I'll give you a piece of my mind old Turk,
        Port Admiral, you be d—d!"

Like the sail-driven warship so aptly portrayed
in their pages, the works of Marryat will possibly
soon sink into undeserved oblivion, and yet they
form most interesting reading, for by their help
the most inattentive reader cannot fail to realize
the vast changes wrought in naval conditions
between the days of Nelson and our own times.
The horny-handed shellbacks of his day would
stare aghast at the intricacies of a modern
battleship and recoil in pardonable consternation
from the roar of her mighty guns.

Though the wind lulled down a trifle towards
evening, it recovered its full strength after

nightfall. Our riding-light resented its violence and refused to burn for long at a time. With a crowd of riding-lights gleaming brightly all around the yacht, there seemed to be no great ground for anxiety. But we went to bed with minds far from completely at rest.

But no blundering newcomer overran the yacht. In the morning the wind was less violent, and it continued gradually to subside. At midday, though none of our neighbours showed any sign of moving, tired of inaction and confident of improved weather, we weighed anchor, and under whole mainsail, ran rapidly out by the E. entrance. There was a touch of N. in the wind which gave the yacht a broad reach in smooth water across Bigbury bay. But, before Bolt Tail was reached, we discovered that our sanguine view of the weather was an entirely unwarranted assumption. The wind piped up venomously and speedily persuaded us to tie down a couple of reefs in the mainsail. That done, we considered our further movements. We seemed to have the choice of two alternatives—to return to Plymouth or to fight our way into Salcombe; we chose the latter.

Nor had we much difficulty in making our port of refuge. Under Bolt head the usual squalls swooped down upon us despitefully and the wind poured from the river as through the mouth of a funnel, but the water in the bay was smooth and grew smoother every yard the yacht advanced. We fetched across to the E. side and then, on starboard tack, were soon up to the bar. The tide was low and we were doubtful of sufficient water, consequently we fell easy victims to the solicitation of a pilot. His name was Foale. He worked the yacht to a berth just above the town, relieved us of the trouble of taking away the kedge and charged us 6s. for pilotage. For hours we had been cursing the folly that had hurried us too soon away from Plymouth; once inside and safely moored, we rejoiced exceedingly in the folly that had brought us to a fresh and beautiful anchorage.

The thorough exploration of Salcombe was left till a later visit. That it is a charming place, every one who has visited it will at once admit. No small cruiser ought to pass Salcombe by. It has a builder's yard, a sailmaker's loft, and several shops of unexpected excellence. One April, twenty years ago, we purchased at one of them for 6d., a dozen new-laid eggs, and they proved to be really what they professed to be—which is not the universal experience of the egg-purchaser. How changed are present times, when eggs of doubtful age but undoubted staleness cost the harassed housekeeper anything from 3½d. to 6d each!

We looked out early and found a gentle E.N.E. wind, but such buffeting had we undergone of late that we did not hurry away before the day had time to give a hint of its probable character. We refused Foale's pressing offer to pilot us out, and at 8 a.m., after a slow drag against a flood-tide, we crossed the bar without difficulty. With smooth water and wind abeam, the yacht was soon abreast of the picturesque ruggedness of Prawle point.

Once out of the bay, we fell in with a very troublesome tidal sea. The wind grew somewhat lighter and the yacht would have been much happier with the topsail set. But the motion was so violent and irregular, and the deck forward so heavily flooded with solid water, that it seemed only prudent to postpone the work of setting it till a quieter area had been reached. An E. running stream, fortunately, hurried us fast to windward. Two miles E. of the Start we tacked and stood towards Dartmouth, soon leaving behind us the tidal rip in which the yacht had been wallowing. The wind fell very light and flawed about wildly. For hours we lay becalmed abreast of Dartmouth. At 4 p.m. a little breeze arose from S. which soon settled down W. by S. The yacht's head was put E. by S. for Portland. Our intention of spending the night in Dartmouth was immediately changed on the arrival of a fair wind.

The wind was light, but blew steadily till 9 p.m. After two hours' calm it came from S.W. Soon after midnight Portland high light was sighted. Two hours later the low light hove up above the horizon. Many owners of small yachts are inclined to shrink from the 50 miles of water that lie between Portland and the Start. But, so far as my experience goes, there is no need for shrinking. Several prolonged passages can be recalled, but I cannot recall a single bad one made in either direction. At 6 a.m. the yacht was off Portland Bill, a mile or two outside the race. Rain had been falling for some time and the land in the general murkiness was barely distinguishable. Breakfast had been prepared and was on the table when the wind received such an accession to its strength that drastic reduction of canvas could not be postponed for a moment. While the mate brought the yacht to the wind, I busied myself in lowering the topsail.

The wet sheet slipped through my fingers, and before the slack could be hauled taut, the slatting of the sail wound it quite securely round the end of the gaff. Nor could it be cleared until the mainsail was lowered sufficiently for the gaff to be reached. The topsail off, we turned our attention to the big jib. This sail never quite carried either of us overboard, but its manipulation in anything of a breeze demanded the greatest care and agility. Having set the storm jib, we proceeded at our leisure to put two reefs in the mainsail. During the tying of the reef points the yacht, by some perverse ingenuity, managed to come about against the backed staysail. We could only listen glumly to the rattle and crash of crockery which betrayed a breakfast wasted on the cabin floor. It was 8 a.m. before the yacht was on her way again. The Shambles lightship showed up dimly to leeward; the land was all concealed in the thickness of the rain.

The strong S.W. wind and favouring tide hurried the yacht along. By 11 a.m. she was off St. Alban's head. The Race was playfully vicious, but we were soon through the worst of this fretful piece of water. The rain ceased and the weather cleared. The sun shone forth and lighted ahead the gleaming chalk cliffs of the Wight. At 1 p.m. with a drain of E. running stream beneath her, the yacht slipped past the Needles. Soon the wind lulled and the tide changed. Though we shook out the reefs and set again topsail and big jib, our progress became steadily slower and slower. Our hope of anchoring off Wootton creek before dark seemed likely to be disappointed. The yacht was just E. of Yarmouth when the wind fell so light that we edged across towards the mainland shore with the intention of anchoring, if necessary, in Lyminton Roads.

But our hearts were cheered and our hopes raised by the blowing at intervals of fickle breezes all the afternoon. At 6 p.m. when we were off the mouth of the Beaulieu river, a steady breeze piped up from right ahead. The tide was slack.

We determined to adhere to our intention of bringing up off Wootton creek. When once we had worked through Cowes Roads and weathered Old Castle point, the yacht lay comfortably along the land on the port tack. We crossed Osborne bay and began to keep a sharp look-out for the entrance to the creek. The night was very dark, and in the absence of leading light of any kind, we soon realized that the attainment of our object would be a task of considerable difficulty. At last, about 10 p.m., under our lee, we made out a break in the solid darkness of the shore. Quite sure that we had found the creek, and thinking that we were unnecessarily far off the land, we lowered the mainsail and jib and ran in quietly under staysail alone. A cast of the lead gave us 3 fathoms. While the staysail was being lowered, the yacht ran firmly ashore.

A dreadful thought flashed through the minds of both, Wootton Rocks! Greatly perturbed, we felt about with the sweeps, but were soon relieved of anxiety. Nothing could be found but sand or hard mud. The bower anchor and 20 fathoms of chain were taken away. After that we lighted the cabin lamp and consulted tide tables. It was just after low water. Unless it blew a gale, we were not likely to come to any harm. The breeze was fresh but there was no sea. Though the yacht soon floated and swung to her anchor, we decided to lie till daylight before we shifted; in the grey dawn we weighed the anchor, set some canvas and were soon brought up off the creek. A passing fisherman, whom we greeted shamefacedly, comforted us with the information that we were by no means the first to mistake in the dark Kingsquay for Wootton creek.

We bade Cowper farewell, and at 7.30 a.m. on the morning of Wednesday, 2nd September, started for the Ferry. The wind was still E. dead in our teeth, but we could delay no longer. Fair wind or foul, we must hasten home. At 9 a.m. when the yacht was between the Warner and the Nab, drenching rain began to fall, but the wind worked so far S. that the yacht would almost lay her course for the Looe channel. One board we were compelled to make near its entrance. Close by the Pullar buoy the yacht was put upon the starboard tack and was soon pitching and plunging through the short tidal seas for which the Looe channel is justly noted. As soon as she was past the Mixon beacon and in quieter water, the topsail was set and her head put upon an E. by S. bearing for Beachy Head. At 11 a.m. the rain ceased, the wind fell lighter and gradually drew ahead. We made the land off Brighton and proceeded to work along shore.

At 6 p.m. the yacht's head gradually came up and soon, on starboard tack, she was pointing seaward off Beachy Head. The sky looked very unpromising, and as a matter of precaution, the

topsail was pulled down and the second substituted for the big jib. A grand sail was enjoyed
that night. With the wind nicely free and quite
strong enough for her lower canvas, the yacht
dashed buoyantly along through considerable
sea, while the phosphorescent water, stirred to
activity by her passage, outlined her sides and
marked her wake with gleaming radiance. At
11.30 p.m. we passed Beachy Head and at
midnight were close to the Royal Sovereign
lightship.

At 5 a.m. Dungeness was abeam. The wind had
lulled and heavy rain was falling. But by 8 a.m.
the tide had carried the yacht abreast of Dover.
A fine S.S.W. wind swept away the rain and
brought us by 1 p.m. to the North Foreland. The
yacht's head was put N.E., and with the wind
now a strong breeze and dead aft, we ran for the
Kentish Knock lightship. At 5 p.m. this was
passed and we ran on with greater comfort now
that, owing to a more N. course, the wind was
slightly on the port quarter. The breeze continued
strong and the sea was heavy.

Throughout the cruise the yacht had been
hampered with the drag of a dinghy astern. It
had been a constant anxiety and a source of
some danger, for, more than once, boarding it
to bail out its cargo of water, I had narrowly
escaped being shot out over the stern. Earlier
in the year we had lost a dinghy off Beachy Head,

the shattered remains of which were picked up at Shoreham. A new boat was built to replace the loss, though scheme after scheme was tried, no method of carrying it on deck could be contrived. It towed well, and, in ordinary weather, could be relied upon to behave with becoming discretion, but when a yacht is running in a heavy sea, the mildest tempered dinghy that ever responded to the pull of the painter is sure, in time, to be guilty of some breach of good manners. Ours suddenly showed that she was no exception to the general rule and gave a remarkable display of petulant waywardness.

The Long Sand Head lightship was broad abeam. I had finished my tea below, lighted a pipe at my ease, and was in the act of stepping into the cockpit to relieve the mate at the tiller, when the dinghy rang up the curtain to give a special performance of her own. Like a destroyer bent on ramming a submarine, she came racing on the top of a sea towards the yacht's stern, just short of her quarry she changed her mind and fell off athwart our wake, with the painter beneath her bottom, for a second or two she rocked idly and seemed as pleased with herself as a puppy that has killed a kitten, she had time, even, to bring herself exactly stern on to the yacht, the sudden jerk of the tautened painter hove her over till a capsize appeared to be inevitable, but when she was half-full of water,

"Senorita," Skipper abaft shrouds

she managed to right herself and followed in our train a very shamefaced and chastened dinghy. This erratic frowardness destroyed any lingering hesitation about doing away with a dinghy altogether. For many years after the *Senorita* carried a Berthon boat; when that was worn out, a pram, built by Jackett of Falmouth, was happily substituted. For a small yacht unable to stow an ordinary dinghy on deck, I cannot conceive a more useful or convenient tender.

The weight she was dragging astern retarded seriously the speed of the yacht, and it was 10 p.m. before the anchor was let go half-way between the Cork lightship and the mouth of the Deben. Ebb tide and darkness rendered impossible immediate entrance. The distance from Wootton creek to our anchorage, more than 160 miles, had been done in less than thirty-nine hours. The next morning we slipped quietly into the river. The cruise was over, but, with the optimistic assurance of youth, before they parted, skipper and mate were already discussing their plans for the following summer.

4

FELIXSTOWE FERRY TO HAVRE AND PLYMOUTH

"Our brows are bound with spindrift and the weed is on
  our knees,
Our loins are battered 'neath us by the swinging, smoking
  seas,
From reef and rock and skerry—over headland, ness, and
  voe—
The Coastwise Lights of England watch the ships of
  England go."

KIPLING.

A T the end of July, slipping away from Woodbridge with a fair wind in a falling tide,
we safely threaded the devious way between the
extensive mud banks, and anchored at Felixstowe
Ferry without adventure of any kind, happy in
the consciousness of labour thrown aside for many
weeks, and of freedom to obey the imperious
summons of the sea.

Monday, 2nd August.—The yacht slipped over
the bar at 10 a.m. against the flood-tide. There
was a good N.W. breeze and a dull sky. We shaped
a course to pass out to the Swin, thence between
the Long Sand and the Shipwash, and round the
Kentish Knock to the N. Foreland. This is a

tricky passage in any but the clearest weather.
The course from the Deben to the Kentish Knock
is about south, but, owing to strong athwart
running tides, a direct course can never be
steered. It is at least 15 miles shorter than the
route by the Thames. But many skippers of
coasters regard the passage with disfavour. They
argue that, if the tides are worked properly, the
Thames route, though longer in distance, will
be shorter in time. Carry the flood, they say, to the
Mouse lightship, and the ebb will hurry the vessel
to the N. Foreland. It seems impudent to pit
amateur experience against professional knowledge, but, bound westward from the neighbourhood of Harwich, I prefer to go "acrost the Kent."

Near the Sunk lightship, 8 miles from the land,
the wind breezed up so strongly that we were
obliged to pull down the topsail. Our outlook was
soon hampered by mist and drizzling rain.
Conditions for our passage could not have been
much worse. We were fortunate in blundering
upon the Long Sand Head bell buoy. That sighted,
we bore away a point to counteract the force of
the ebb tide. We found the Kentish Knock lightship right under our bows, and, free from anxiety,
we put the yacht's head S.W. for the N. Foreland.

Late in the afternoon the rain ceased. The
breeze held up well, but, checked by the strong
ebb, the yacht did not pass the N. Foreland till
7 p.m. As darkness approached, the wind fell

very light. Astern, the Foreland's occulting light seemed to mock us with a leering wink. As we passed slowly through the Gull Stream, we could not detect a single riding-light throughout the whole length of the Downs. One reads in the ballad of *Black-eyed Susan* the line :

"All in the Downs the fleet was moor'd,"

but never again is a crowd of sailing vessels likely to be seen at anchor there, sheltering from a gale or awaiting a fair wind. Soon from the ill-found tramp alone will the Deal hovellers win a precarious living and the Goodwin Sands exact their toll of lives.

Tuesday, 3rd.—The N.W. wind carried us by 10 a.m. abreast of Eastbourne. Then a flat calm fell on the waters. Before noon a W.S.W. breeze of topsail strength set us beating onwards past Beachy Head and its sister heights. Short boards were made along the foot of these stupendous cliffs of gleaming chalk. At 7.30 p.m. breeze and favouring tide ended together and the yacht was anchored off Shoreham.

Wednesday, 4th.—At 4 a.m. we found a little S.E. wind blowing. The anchor was weighed at once. About 9.30 a.m. the Owers lightship hove in sight. The great mass of the Owers Shoal, a group of rocky patches extending 5 miles S.E. from Selsea Bill, is separated from Selsea Bill by the Looe and must at some age of the world's history have formed part of the mainland. The tide was pouring against the yacht, and the wind died away to the faintest of breezes. At 2.30 p.m. we dragged past the lightship. Her crew launched a boat and brought us letters to post. Many a letter, in her time, has the *Senorita* conveyed to the postman for the grateful watchers on outlying lightships. At 3 p.m. a W.S.W. air arose which carried us over a now propitious tide to the Nab lightship. An E. running stream was pouring out of Spithead. At 7.30 p.m. we anchored for the night in St. Helen's Roads.

The next morning the yacht was worked only so far as Wootton creek, where we renewed our acquaintance with Cowper, who volunteered to accompany us on the trip across the Channel to Havre.

Monday, 9th.—With wind W., inclined to soften, the yacht ran out of the creek soon after 3 p.m. With tide beneath her she slipped quietly past Ryde, Bembridge, and Culver Cliff. The course was S. by E., and the distance 90 miles. Before dark the wind was gone. Thick fog. Steam-boats, passing either way, gave us an anxious time. The shriek of sirens and the blare of our fog-horn prevented the watch below from enjoying much sound sleep.

Tuesday, 10th.—Shortly after midnight the fog lifted. At 1 a.m. a gentle breeze, E.S.E., enabled the yacht to lay her course. Before 3 a.m. we had some showers of rain. The clouds brought up heavy puffs, but as the wind lulled down again we kept the topsail aloft. At 6 a.m. it was raining heavily and there was not a breath of wind. The sea was sloppy, and the yacht rolled helplessly. We had a very trying time till 10 a.m., when a W.N.W. breeze brought comfort, and a beautiful day began. The yacht ran on rapidly before growing sea. At 4 p.m. land was made out on our port bow, and, a little later, we were able to decide that it was Cap La Hève, which, rising high to the E. of the entrance, guides with its light the shipping of all nations into the rapid waters of the river Seine. By this time it was blowing so that the topsail could be carried no longer.

Now that we had made a good landfall, and were sure of shelter of some sort before dark, the possibility was keenly debated of running to Trouville rather than to Havre. The former, with its mixed bathing—as yet almost unknown on English shores—its casino, *petits chevaux* and gay follies of a fashionable watering-place, seemed likely to give more amusement than could be derived from a sober inspection of the lofty buildings and commercial prosperity of a big port. Trouville was by far the more alluring. But the falling tide, a heavy sea, a rising wind, and the approach of night gave us ample ground to hesitate before deciding in its favour. "Better be sure than sorry," quoth the skipper of a barge once in my hearing, as he compelled a reluctant mate to take away the kedge. Simple words that embody a world of wisdom! Havre is a port easy to enter. Trouville, with its miles of outlying sands dry at low water, is not a place to be tackled lightly by strangers under unfavourable conditions. Listening to the dictates of prudence, we ran on to Havre, gybed as we passed between the pier heads, and made fast to a smack lying alongside a quay near the first lock-gates on the left. We congratulated ourselves on securing a comfortable berth outside the confines of an objectionable *bassin*.

But before our evening meal was over, a polite but firmly worded intimation was conveyed to us that we must shift at once from our present quarters. The lock-gates were open, but, desiring at all costs to avoid a *bassin*, an effort was made under stay-sail to reach a mooring-buoy lying out in the harbour. The strong wind and a drain of tide swept the yacht away from her aim. Dead to leeward lay the buttresses of another lock-gate. Nothing much short of a miracle could save the yacht from being dashed upon their cruel fronts. The mainsail was covered up, the Berthon dinghy lay collapsed on deck, not a boat was near to give assistance; before sail could be made she would be foul of the buttresses. We thrust out the sweeps. By gigantic exertions we managed to fetch a lighter lying to a buoy.

As a clock was striking 6 a.m. the next morning, we were aroused by the arrival of a boat along-side. The ancient mariner on board it advised our instant departure, for a liner was due to enter. The *bassin* was evidently our destiny, and it seemed useless to struggle any longer against the inevitable. By 8 a.m. we were inside, in a comfortable enough berth, next to an Irish yacht which a few days before had crossed over from Kinsale. A dock at home is rarely a pleasant resting place for a yacht; a dock abroad gives, usually, an even less delectable harbourage. Experience alone will unfold its full catalogue of horrors.

Thursday, 12th.—Havre has fine docks, crowded with shipping, but offers little of interest to the passing stranger. We determined to re-cross the Channel, and continue our voyage westward. With some difficulty the harbour was cleared at 9 a.m. Outside there was a gentle W.S.W. wind. The sea was heavy, but once past Cap La Hève, we found it less troublesome. With topsail and big jib, we set our course for the Wight. The wind remained very light, and backed persistently. But the day was beautifully warm and fine. At 6 p.m. Cape Antifer was still in sight. Soon after 9 p.m. a gentle S. wind came, which gradu-ally veered to S.W., and increased in force. Rain

clouds blew up with accompanying squalls.
In the afternoon it occurred to us that the yacht
had escaped from France without paying any
charges either to the dock, or the *douane*. There
was no desire on our part to defraud any one of
their legitimate dues. We had forgotten all about
them, and the authorities had apparently overlooked us.

Friday, 13*th*.—At midnight we hesitated about
stowing the topsail, but decided to let it stand.
It was my watch below. I lay listening to the rush
of water past my ear, expecting every moment
a call to reduce canvas. At 1.30 a.m., in drenching
rain, the topsail was hauled down, and a couple
of reefs put in the mainsail. The big jib had to be
changed. Those were the days of long bowsprits
and lofty topmasts (1886). The *Senorita's* big jib
was a large sail, cut low on the foot. It was no
light armful to manage on the narrow and sloping
space available. The mate and myself had a
terrible struggle with it on this occasion, but that
off and the storm-jib set, we scrambled aft
breathless and wet through. In theory the topmast could be housed without the help of a hand
aloft. A tripping line pulled the fid into a position
that allowed the topmast to slip down by its own
weight. In practice, except at anchor, the arrange-
ment always failed on the *Senorita*. None of us
feeling inclined to shin aloft in the wind and the
wet, the topmast was left on end. By no one

was the advent of the pole-mast and shortened
bowsprit hailed with greater appreciation than
by myself.

Just before daylight St. Catherine's light was
sighted right ahead. The strong wind soon carried
the yacht under the lee of the Wight. In smoother
water she ran on rapidly. The rain ceased and the
wind fell light. On the edge of Ryde Sand we
shook out the reefs and, though the water was
scant and the channel narrow, we worked up
Wootton Creek without touching the mud. The
moorings were picked up soon after 7 a.m. That
evening we bade our genial host farewell.

Saturday, 14*th*.—With light breeze, N.N.W. and
weather misty, the yacht slipped out of the creek
at 10.30 a.m. on the first of the W. going tide.
There was little wind all day. The Needles were
passed at 1.45 p.m. At 6 p.m., off Holdfast point,
with wind W.S.W., light, we tacked seawards.
We had a fine view of the twin chalk pinnacles,
known as old Harry and his Wife.

Sunday, 15*th*.—At midnight the yacht was off
Anvil point, on starboard tack, headed S., with
every stitch of canvas set. The S.W. wind was
light but steady, and the *Senorita* cleft her way
merrily through the little wavelets that sought
rather to kiss the cheeks of the intruder than to
impede her passage through their midst. At 5 a.m.
she was wallowing about in a calm, outside the
race, off Portland Bill. Wallowing in a seaway

suggests no poetic fancies. It is an unmitigated abomination. Two hours later the yacht was on the port tack heading N.W. and W.N.W. The day was cold with a crisp breeze. The wind steadily grew stronger, and at 2 p.m. the topsail was stowed. At 5 p.m. Berry head was sighted on our port bow. There was then a lot of wind, a nasty sea, and a very ugly sky. We changed jibs and put two reefs in the mainsail. It was determined to take refuge in Dartmouth till the unpleasant weather was overpast, and we worked painfully and slowly towards the desired haven, which lay to windward. At 8 p.m. a pall of soaking thickness settled down, and the blackest of black nights began. Shortly before midnight we were somewhere in the neighbourhood of Dartmouth, but were unable to pick up the leading lights. The yacht was hard pressed by a very strong wind, and our efforts to gain the shelter of the harbour were not lightly abandoned. But, at last, unable to see our way, suspicious of the smoothness of the water, which showed that the land was close aboard, unwilling to court disaster by approaching too nearly the outlying dangers of unknown shores, we were constrained, thoroughly tired though we were and far from happy, to lay the yacht to till daylight.

We took the third reef in the mainsail and stowed the stay-sail. With the spit-fire jib hauled slightly to windward, and the mainsail sheeted in fairly taut, the yacht lay quietly, bowing and curtseying to the sea, which grew heavier the farther she was blown off the land. This was nearly our first experience of lying-to under compulsion. After hours of pitching and plunging and being swept fore and aft by floods of water, the quiet and dry produced a feeling of great comfort and speedily removed all sense of anxiety. It was soon found that the yacht might be left to her own devices. On starboard tack she could not come foul of the land. We changed our sopping garments, had a big meal, and, in turn, a few hours' sleep. The man on duty kept most of his watch in the cabin, thrusting his head out at frequent intervals to see that no vessel was near enough to trouble our peace.

Monday, 16*th.*—Start point showed up white and sharply defined against the slate-coloured sky. It bore W., distant 6 or 7 miles. At 6 a.m. the wind was much less and good enough to allow the yacht to head direct for Dartmouth. We shook out a reef, set the staysail, and made straight for the harbour. The big seas, regular and true, in no way hampered the yacht. As she drew near the land the wind headed her off and she failed to fetch the Mewstone. We made a board. On port tack once more, a fierce squall hurried us into the very entrance—and then left us to the mercy of fitful puffs flawing from all directions. A brief trial showed conclusively that all efforts to pass St. Petrox church against the tide would be unavailing. We refused the offer of a tug to tow us in, bore away and at 10.45 a.m. dropped anchor in the Range in good shelter.

At 2 p.m. the anchor was weighed, and the yacht worked up to a berth a little way above the *Britannia*. We had a turn ashore in the evening. Dartmouth is a quaint old town, and the river and its surroundings are picturesque enough to arouse the enthusiastic admiration of every beholder, but I must confess to not feeling any great liking for the place. The harbour is usually difficult to enter, and equally difficult to leave, on account of the baffling flaws in the wind caused by the high ground on either side of the narrow entrance. By nightfall the breeze had blown itself out, but the sky showed little sign of more settled weather.

Tuesday, 17th.—It was only a moderate sort of morning but we determined to try to reach Plymouth. Wind W.N.W. At 10.25 a.m. the yacht cleared the harbour and ran, with sheets eased up, inside the Skerries down to the Start. At 11.45 a.m. we hauled our wind round the point, and found a stiff N.W. wind blowing. A choppy sea kept our decks very wet, but a W. running tide soaked us quickly to windward. The wind became so strong that reefing appeared to be a course of immediate necessity, but it lulled again, and we let the yacht plunge on under whole mainsail. After a long cast off we fetched, on our port tack, to windward of Bolt Tail well into Bigbury bay and smoother water. The breeze, drawing off the land, enabled the yacht for a while to lie up along the shore. But the wind soon came ahead again. At 7 p.m. we slipped past the E. end of Plymouth breakwater into the Sound.

We saw several small craft lying near the pier, under the Hoe. They were all at moorings, and the water in their neighbourhood proved to be deep. It seemed to be an unsuitable place for the yacht. Rounding Drake's Island, we liked the look of Firestone bay, and brought up there. We had, accidentally, hit upon one of the best berths for small craft in the whole of the Sound.

The view of Plymouth Sound always raises a glow of pride in my patriotic breast. It is impossible for a man, in any way acquainted with the history of the Elizabethan age, to cast his eyes over these waters and remain unmoved. Let him sit on the Hoe, with his face turned towards the sea. In front and to his right are lying now, just as they lay more than 300 years ago, Drake's Island, the entrance to the Hamoaze, Mount Edgcumbe, and Penlee, with Cawsand bay tucked in between; to his left, the high land E. of the Sound and Sutton Pool. The topographical features remain unchanged.

It requires no great powers of imagination to picture the old sea-captains, in the quaint garb of the period, finishing their game of bowls on the turf somewhere behind him, to picture the clumsy vessels of 1588, creeping on the first of the ebb out of the Hamoaze and Sutton Pool, to sail off in pursuit of the unwieldy Spanish fleet, that has for hours been passing slowly across the view of the anxious throngs ashore. Ah, the brave days of old! oh, to have lived in the reign of the Virgin Queen! when a young man, with naught to back him save his good sword and strong right arm, might carve a road to fame and fortune—a simpler age, in which we can imagine men living happier lives than in these later days, untrammelled by the conventions of our more complex civilisation,

> "Because the good old rule
> Sufficeth them—the simple plan
> That they should take who have the power
> And they should keep who can."
>
> WORDSWORTH.

III

TO SCILLY : BACK TO THE DEBEN

"Come up, come in from Eastward, from the guard posts of
   the morn!
Beat up, beat in from Southerly, Oh gipsies of the Horn!
Swift shuttles of an Empire's loom that weave us, main
   to main,
The Coastwise Lights of England give you welcome back
   again!"

KIPLING.

AT PLYMOUTH. *Wednesday*, 18*th August*.—
Anchor was weighed at 8 a.m., and with
a light N.W. wind, the yacht ran slowly through
the sound, the surface of which was ruffled only
by the breaking of shoals of mackerel. Outside
the wind was found to be W.S.W. and somewhat
stronger. We passed close to windward of the
Liverpool barque, *Annie Story*, which had been
towed out ahead of the yacht. All day we worked
westward with light wind and smooth water. At
6 p.m. under our lee bow lay Gribben head,
conspicuous by reason of its lofty beacon tower.
Feeling lazy and expecting a calm night, we bore
away for Fowey, and, at 7.30 p.m., the yacht
was anchored off Polruan. This was the first of
many visits to Fowey. It is a delightful place,

though a dyspeptic visitor from the Midlands is reported to have grumbled that the sole apparent attractions of Fowey were Q.'s house, Q. himself, and Q.'s books. With the first two I am unacquainted; the last are a joy to every one who knows anything of Cornwall and the Cornish. To the man detained at Fowey by bad weather or other causes, the *Tale of Troy Town* can be recommended. Its perusal will lighten much of the tedium generated by his confinement to the harbour and send him exploring in the dinghy the upper waters of the river.

Tuesday, 19*th*.—Some necessary provisioning delayed our start. It was 10.30 a.m. before the yacht was clear of Gribben head and the Cannis Rock, a nasty reef, in those days still unmarked by a beacon (1886). There was a fresh N.W. breeze, but she could carry all her lower canvas. We started with the intention of making Scilly without entering any intermediate port. Rapidly the yacht left St. Austell bay astern, in the recesses of which lie the two dry harbours of Charlestown and Par, both devoted to the export of China clay and quite unsuitable for the harbourage of yachts. We passed the fishing port of Mevagissey and the Guineas Rocks, and were nearing the bulky mass of the Dodman when the wind fell lighter and we sent the topsail aloft. We rounded the Dodman and opened Black head and the line of coast west of the bay at the

5

N. end of which lies the noble harbour of Falmouth.

At 4 p.m. we passed farther seaward of the Lizard than we desired. About the Stag Rocks were numbers of boats, manned by strong crews hauling their lobster-pots. These rocks are an unnecessary and dangerous extension of a noble headland.

At 5 p.m. we tacked towards the land. At 7 p.m. the yacht was put again upon the starboard tack and could just lay the course W. by N.½N. for St. Mary's Sound in Scilly. The wind gradually improved in direction till it blew directly upon our starboard beam. The sea was perfectly smooth. As we had entered into strange waters, we stowed the topsail and substituted the second for the big jib.

Wednesday, 20th.—At midnight the moon was peeping fitfully between the clouds. Immediately around us there was no fog, but ahead there stretched across our path a curtain of dense blackness. At 1.30 a.m., when the Lizard lights were sinking astern, the yacht ran into a thick fog. We peered, but peered in vain, for the light on the Wolf Rock. This reef, 60 yards long by 50 yards broad, a mere pin's head on the surface of deep waters—*dorsum immane mari summo*—lurked a hidden danger for many an unsuspicious mariner in the days before a lighthouse was painfully erected upon its restricted plateau. In these later times, the alternating flashes of red and white, shot from the lighthouse, guide to safety the unending stream of traffic that pours along the narrow passage between Land's End and the Seven Stones lightship. The distance from the Lizard to Scilly is 44 miles. The Wolf Rock lies about half-way. Our failure to sight its light was somewhat disconcerting, for the only assistance we now had to our navigation was the sound of the fog signal on the Longships, off Land's End. Its double explosive report, reverberating every five minutes, loudly, at first, on our starboard bow, gradually came abeam, and passed with diminishing sound over our quarter, and was finally lost completely astern.

At 5 a.m. the wind was lighter and the fog more dense. We knew that we must be nearing Scilly, and were thankful that the yacht was not dashing forward at a great pace. A little later we could smell the land, and hear the shriek of birds wrangling, as they will from pure delight in wrangling, and the boom of billows breaking upon a not far distant shore. It was, undoubtedly, time to lie-to, and await the lifting of the fog. As I was stepping below to try to derive some information from a further inspection of the chart, an object suddenly loomed up upon our starboard bow.

"Look out!" I yelled to the mate at the tiller. "Here's a vessel right on top of us!"

A moment later we saw that it was not a vessel but a pinnacle of rock rising abruptly from the water. Then other pinnacles showed. With our hearts in our mouths we gybed the yacht all standing on to the port tack. The fog suddenly lifted. Yonder was St. Agnes' lighthouse, dead to windward, two or three miles distant, and we shuddered to see astern now—but a moment ago ahead—a miscellaneous collection of lofty pinnacles and low-lying islets, a wide-yawning destruction only barely avoided.

The wind, N. by E., would not allow the yacht to lie up along the land, but a weather-going tide swept her towards St. Mary's Sound.

Influenced chiefly by the near advance of further fog-banks, we hoisted a pilot-jack and anxiously scanned the shore for approaching assistance. At last, when the yacht was breast of the lighthouse, we saw a boat put off from St. Agnes. Eager to have some one on board acquainted with these waters, before we were enveloped by the fog now fast swirling down, we tacked and ran towards the boat. It was a keen race between the fog and the yacht. In sporting parlance, the yacht won by a short head. Billowing wreaths, the advance guard of a dense bank, were already swirling round the yacht when a young fisherman stepped on board who undertook to pilot us to Hugh Town in St. Mary for the modest fee of five shillings.

Hardly was his boat made fast when we became aware of loud hailing. Dimly through the fog was made out a boat ahead, carrying a flag on a staff at its stern. On board it was the Trinity House pilot. With our eyes fixed upon the other boat, we had failed to notice his approach. He boarded us and turned out the unlicensed interloper, who departed with 2s. in his pocket but wrath in his language. By some means the pilot —Abraham James Hicks—found his way into St. Mary's Sound, which separates St. Agnes from its near neighbour St. Mary. The yacht had just passed the Spanish Ledge buoy when the fog disappeared, the sun came out hot, and the wind fell very light. It was 10 a.m. before we reached St. Mary's Pool, where we picked up a pilot-boat's moorings. Pilotage amounted to a sovereign, the smallest charge that could be made. We had an uneasy suspicion that advantage was being taken of our innocence. But we paid up without demur and with as good a grace as we could assume.

We remained two days at Scilly, and went the usual round of sight-seeing.

Monday, *23rd*.—It was a very thick morning with a light N. wind. When, at 11 a.m., the fog lifted somewhat, we slipped our moorings, and, having passed through St. Mary's Sound, shaped a course E. by S. southerly for the Lizard. It struck us this morning, with a slight shock, that the days were passing rapidly, and that the yacht was far from her winter home. We determined to try to gain on time by making an unbroken run to the Wight. The weather was dull and rather cold. There was no actual fog, but the horizon was drawn very closely round the yacht. She slipped along quietly all day. Again nothing was seen of the Wolf Rock or of the land. For a couple of hours, just before dark, the wind fell very light. Then came a fine W.N.W. breeze which sent the yacht along fast upon her course.

The lights in our binnacle had never been a success. The oil employed was colza, the most unsatisfactory of all illuminants, but the only one, so far, in general use for sea-going lamps. We had done everything possible to woo the fickle flame to remain alight. Time after time the carefully trimmed wicks were lighted in the shelter of the cabin, only to flicker out the moment the oil containers were enclosed in the lamps. If the lamps refused to burn in the cabin, how could they be expected to burn in the binnacle? Such was our argument, but this night we changed our tactics. The lamps were lighted, shut up, and thrust into the binnacle without a moment's delay. We were astonished to find that they burned brightly. They had, no doubt, the exact draught of air required. With great relief the big old dry compass, by which we had been accustomed, with difficulty, to steer through the hours of darkness, was put away below for good.

The wind blew strong and steady, the water was beautifully smooth. At 10.30 p.m. there glared out ahead a light of greenish tinge which appeared to be a vessel's starboard sidelight. The yacht was luffed a little to go clear. The light was lost immediately and, thinking that all risk was over of contact with the nearing vessel, I put her upon the course again. Then two lights suddenly shone out ahead, high up in the air. The Lizard! We were ahead of our reckoning— an unusual occurrence. An envelope of mist must have concealed the lights from my vision, for we were so close to the land that the outline of the cliffs could be seen distinctly. The yacht was run away to avoid the Stag Rocks, the lights brought in one—in those days the Lizard had two lighthouses—opened again, and by 11 p.m., thanks to a strong fair tide, we were round the head, and laying our course E. for the Eddystone. It grew very dark, some rain fell, and the wind piped up, but at midnight, when the mate took charge, we determined to keep the topsail aloft a while longer. It was felt, now that the Lizard was astern, that the yacht had once more entered sheltered waters and that, if the girls at home had their hands on the tow-rope, it was only fair that we should play our part to second their efforts.

Tuesday, 24*th*.—At 1.30 a.m. we were obliged

to take in the topsail, but we left the big jib
standing. It seemed a pity to waste any of the
gallant breeze and what sea there was, well on
the beam, neither swept the yacht nor endangered
the bowsprit. At 3 a.m. it was cold and miserable
on deck. There was a lot of wind and a threat of
more. The yacht was edged in somewhat towards
the land to obtain smoother water. At 7 a.m. she
was speeding along with the Eddystone, 2 or
3 miles off, broad on her starboard beam. Mist
hung over the land, but Plymouth Mewstone was
sighted. The yacht's head was put S.E. to run
for the Start. The sun came out and dissipated
the mist. Our forecast of strong breezes proved
painfully ill-founded. Instead of breezing up, the
wind lulled down, and the topsail was re-set.
At 11 a.m., off Bolt head, the wind failed entirely.
From a sky destitute of cloud, the sun poured
down upon us almost tropical heat.

A faint S.E. air carried us past Prawle point.
After its departure not the faintest breeze stirred
the waters till 8 p.m., by which time a fleet of
between twenty and thirty sail, of all rigs and
sizes, had drifted up into our neighbourhood.
The tide swept us all slowly towards the Start.
The coast scenery hereabouts is fine ; but the
finest scenery soon fails to counterpoise the
irritation caused by a protracted calm.

Even calms have their limits. Soon after 8 p.m.
there came a breeze W.N.W. It lasted but a few

minutes, and left the yacht tumbling about in a tidal swabble, just E. of the Start.

Wednesday, 25*th*.—It was a magnificent night, such a night as never entirely fades from a man's memory.

At 5 a.m. the yacht was off the Bill, at a convenient distance outside the race. Soon the wind lulled.

Between Durlstone head and Swanage a crack was heard aloft. Lifting our eyes in the direction of the sound, we saw the quiet descent of the throat of the mainsail. The hook of the upper main-halyard block had parted. With the wind well astern we could with deliberation set about repairs.

The breeze continued strong and true. At 2 p.m., with a fair tide underneath her, the yacht passed the Needles. At 4 p.m. the anchor was let go off Wootton. As the yacht was brought to the wind, many cracks were heard aloft, but our lashing held. The local blacksmith repaired the block very skilfully at a trifling charge.

This run of 200 miles occupied exactly fifty-three hours, during nine of which the yacht was lying becalmed near the Start. Except for a short time on Tuesday morning, the topsail was carried the whole way. It was one of the pleasantest runs ever made in the *Senorita*.

Monday, 30*th*.—We started soon after noon with a S.E. wind, bound for Felixstowe Ferry. The

tide was still running to the westward, and the
wind came due E. Prospects were far from favourable. Once started, we were determined to carry
through our design, and our determination was
pleasantly rewarded. After a spell of calm, near
the Warner lightship, the wind came away
S.S.W. With great cheerfulness we trimmed our
sheets and from the Nab sailed the yacht E.S.E.
for the Looe. With a fair tide and nice breeze she
slipped along fast. About 4.30 p.m., at a very
inopportune moment, sudden and unexpected
fog fell upon us. It might well have delayed its
coming till we had passed through the difficulties
of the narrow channel in front. However, all
anxiety was removed by our discovery to windward of the Pullar buoy lying on its side, and a
little later to leeward, of the Dries buoy, a more
upstanding mark. We held on confidently, and
soon put the yacht upon the course E. by S. for
Beachy Head.

I was sleepily waiting for the time to call up
the mate when my senses were suddenly startled
into wakefulness by hearing in our immediate
neighbourhood the voices of men talking together.

Peering in the direction whence the sound proceeded, I made out dimly on my port bow the
apparent glare of a riding-light. There happened
to be at the moment a little air, and the yacht
was steered a point to seawards to give the light

a good berth. She astonished me by refusing to answer the helm. Her head came round to S. and stuck on that bearing; she would neither luff up nor bear away. A peculiar rippling made me look over the side. A line of phosphorescence stretched away at an angle of 45° from either bow. The yacht was held up by a drift net, and the light shone, no doubt, from the forestay of a boat riding to it. Though a net is, according to an Irishman's definition, but " a lot of holes tied up wid sthring," it is wonderfully retentive. The mate, called on deck in a whisper, tried with the butt end of the boat-hook to push the rope of the net beneath our fore-foot. His efforts met with no immediate success, but, just as I was about to hail the boat, we found ourselves free. The yacht drifted away in the fog and the light disappeared in a moment.

Tuesday, 31st.—The mate had not a breath of wind all his watch. At 3. am. the draughts seemed to be from E., but it was too faint to allow us to decide with certainty its exact direction. The sound of surf was audible to port. The fog was very dense. An invisible vessel drifted past to starboard. She gave a good-humoured little blast upon her fog-horn.

After 5 a.m. the mate in charge of the deck used the fog-horn very freely. There was something big creeping about quite close, he declared. Next he began to talk in a loud voice. Greatly incensed at having my chance of a short sleep destroyed, I thrust my head up the companion just in time to hear a gruff voice from somewhere high above us exclaim:

"You're all right: I can see you."

To hear, apparently from the clouds, the words of an invisible speaker was decidedly uncanny. In answer to my startled inquiries the mate explained that the voice came from the bridge of a steamboat, at the moment, he fancied, a few lengths astern. He had been conversing with the speaker for some little time, but had been unable, so far, to fix his exact bearing. It was comforting to know that the yacht could be seen.

Soon after 7 a.m. a smart E. wind suddenly swept away the fog. Seaford head was found close abeam. Not far astern was a big passenger boat which made off at once for Newhaven. At 10 a.m. we were off Beachy Head.

Wednesday, 1st September.—Shortly before 3 a.m. Dungeness light was sighted. A little breeze carried us safely through a small fleet of vessels anchored between Fairlight and Dungeness, waiting, with canvas set, for the turn of tide. At 5 a.m. it was quite calm and the tide was pouring strongly against the yacht. She was some way inside the line of general traffic. We let go the anchor, and went to sleep straightway. "Sleep! the more sleep ye gets, the more ye want!" was one of Tom Newson's favourite aphorisms, and it contains more truth than many an aphorism from more learned lips.

At 10 a.m. the tide turned to the eastward. A gentle S. breeze brought us to Dungeness by noon. The wind remained very paltry. At 6.30 p.m. the yacht was passing the pier at Dover.

Thursday, 2nd.—By midnight the wind had grown so strong that the topsail could be carried no longer. During the operation of stowing it we flew past the Gull lightship. The wind went round so far that the yacht would barely lay her course N.E.¾N. for the Kentish Knock lightship, but the help of a racing tide was no small advantage. At 3 a.m. she was heading 2 points E. of her course. At 5 a.m. we gave her a cast in on starboard tack. An hour later, soon after we had put her on the port tack again, the lightship was found just under our lee bow. So far, so good! But the wind N.N.E. had fallen very light. Our course onwards, without allowance for the tide soon due to pour westward, was N. by W. A haze had settled down and closely curtailed the range of our eyes. With wind ahead and light, with hazy weather, with a tide pouring like a mill-race athwart our course, the passage to the land was not devoid of difficulty.

But we were not unduly depressed by our difficulties. For hours the yacht made short boards E.N.E. and N.N.W., losing on the latter tack, owing to the lee-going flood, anything

gained on the former. We sighted a buoy bearing
W. This was made out to be the North Knock,
3½ miles from the Kentish Knock lightship. The
lightship had been long lost in the haze, and we
were glad to have in sight something whereby
to fix our position on the chart. At 2 p.m., high
water, we determined to hold on across everything on the starboard tack, feeling confident
that the ebb would sweep the yacht to windward
of the Long Sand. But one more board was
necessary. The mast of a wreck and a patch of
broken water ahead showed that the yacht was
too near the shoal part of the sand. But before
long she was on the starboard tack once more,
heading N.N.W. The wind grew stronger, and,
meeting the ebb now running fiercely, soon raised
a nasty sea.

Crossing the Rough, where the tidal sea was
very malevolent, we received a tremendous
ducking. The tide swept us down nearly to the
Cutler Sand, but, bearing away handsomely,
we found the Deben Fairway buoy, and, with
scant water on the bar and a foaming tide tearing
out, we attempted to pass into the river. But the
yacht touched and the tide taking charge bustled
her out to sea again.

We brought up at a convenient distance from
the shore and slipped into the river in the morning.

I V

"OH, GIVE TO ME THE GOOD OLD DAYS
OF FIFTY YEARS AGO!"

A WIDELY read London daily paper lately allowed its pages to be the medium of a discussion about the ill-defined date of the Good Old Days. From only a slight acquaintance with classical lore it may be inferred that the ancient writers, even in their times, regarded the past as better than the present, and were equally at a loss with modern disputants to fix the exact period of superlative excellence. One of the contributors to the controversy maintained that the happy period unquestionably coincided with the years, when the income tax amounted to no more than 6d. in the £. There is much to be said for his view —but why 6d. when 3d. is a sum no harder to mention and gives a keener point to his argument?

When my small income was first subjected to this inquisitorial demand, the exaction, unless I am greatly mistaken, was limited to 3d. in the £, and the then Chancellor of the Exchequer had the hardihood to assert that under no possible combination of evil circumstances could it ever exceed a modest shilling. No doubt, at the moment he was carried away by the exuberance of his own verbosity, and he was, perhaps, happy in not living long enough to see the deadly falsification of his confident prophecy.

The discussion recalled the words quoted above, drawn from a song much in vogue when—*consule Planco*—my years were yet few. The wish is foolish and, most happily, vain. Most men, who can go back fifty years in their memory, know perfectly well that, except for the enjoyment of irresponsible youth, and the yet unblighted hope of applying to the world an opening knife—quoth the ancient Pistol:

> "Why, then the world's mine oyster,
> Which I with sword will open."

They find the present years neither better nor worse than those that are gone. The present period of insane strikes and Bolshevist activity may be, it is to be hoped, regarded as an exceptional anomaly in the sober sense of our manual labourers.

Anyway, no yachting man has good reason to desire a return to the gear and fittings of the years of traditional superiority. One need only scan the print of a yacht of the time, or gaze upon the paintings of the old craft that decorate the walls of the club, to realize completely the improved conditions that now prevail. The outrageously long bowsprits, towering topmasts, square-headed

"SENORITA," ALL PLAIN SAIL

gaff topsails, huge low-cut jibs—all these, ludicrous as they appear to our eyes, were accepted with complaisance, less than fifty years ago, as nearing the height of unimprovable perfection. But acquiescence in an equipment so overwhelmingly clumsy must be attributed entirely to ignorance of easier simplicity:

> "Where ignorance is bliss
> 'Tis folly to be wise."
>
> GRAY.

The art of reefing a bowsprit is hardly known to the present generation, and the need to practise it now rarely arises, while the loss of bowsprit, except by collision with the wall of a dock or the side of a steamboat, is a misfortune quite outside the range of every day probabilities. But in the old types of yachts, with their bowsprits of inordinate length and their extremities bowsed down to excess, reefing was constantly necessary, and loss was an accident of frequent occurrence. The very weight of the projecting spar increased any tendency in the boat to plunge, and the generous steeve demanded by fashion assisted the weight in inviting disaster. It was a happy day when some defiant iconoclast broke through the trammels of universal custom and fitted his yacht with a stump bowsprit and a diminutive jib. Probably he had to live down the customary mockery of the innovator, but, after losing three bowsprits in two seasons, I became a whole-

6

hearted convert to the novel idea. The bowsprit was shortened and the big jib removed from the sail-locker. On a broad reach its absence detracted a trifle from the speed of the *Senorita*, but the little loss of speed was more than counterbalanced by the comforting certainty that the yacht no longer ran the risk of pitching head first into a heavy sea and of emerging from her dive with decks cleared of all lumber and the bowsprit bobbing up and down alongside to leeward.

The August of 1890 was a miserable month. Out of all the years of my sea-faring of this year alone no record was kept. The why or wherefore goodness only knows. Mere laziness is the most likely explanation. Of the cruise as a whole very little lingers in the memory, but some of its episodes stand forth from the general blank with surprising vividness.

Our first morning out, at daybreak, the *Senorita* was plunging about heavily in a calm at the mouth of the Thames not far from the Tongue lightship. To ease her was impossible, and each plunge presaged the instant doom of the bowsprit. The sunrise was the most startling that my eyes have ever had the luck to observe. Shortly before the sun was due above the horizon, all the N.E. sky was concealed by a curtain of dirty red, flecked by streaks of sickly green and topped by writhing masses of inky blackness. The actual sun did not show its face all day, but some time elapsed before the threatening ruddiness was completely obliterated by dismal clouds of mist and rain. Our expectation of a bad time was filled to the full, and immediately. We had a very heavy dusting. In torrents of rain and a squally S.W. wind, we fought our way stubbornly to Dover and sought shelter in the Granville dock.

And there we remained in morose helplessness for more than a week. When, at last, the weather moderated sufficiently to permit us to proceed, we worked away perseveringly to windward and managed in the end to struggle as far as Salcombe. The subduing of difficulties is one of the aims of a liberal education, but an occasional fair wind gladdens the heart—and gives to the crew an opportunity to dry their wet garments. From Salcombe, with only little time to spare, we started to run back to Woodbridge, the yacht's winter home. Daily we expected our ill-luck to bring an E. wind and to give us a further bout of beating to windward. But our anxiety proved to be uncalled for. The blustering W. winds continued to blow with unexpected persistence.

From the Wight the yacht ran on her way with the wind dead aft. We carried the whole mainsail when a single reef would have been a bare enough reduction in our spread of canvas. To many a young man a superabundance of sail conveys a sense of pure joy rather than of insensate folly.

> "Nought cared this body for wind or weather
> When youth and I lived in't together."
>
> COLERIDGE.

Still, good grounds for carrying on in this instance were not wanting, for the time to return to work was drawing rapidly near. We were lucky enough to escape an involuntary gybe and the consequences that frequently accompany such a serious accident. My recollection of times is, naturally, vague. But at some late hour in the afternoon the yacht passed Beachy Head, and now, that the course shifted slightly to the N., she ran on for Dungeness in less danger of gybing. Off Fairlight, fully persuaded that the night now descending could not fail to be dirty, we took off the staysail and shortened the mainsail by a couple of reefs.

As we rounded Dungeness it was blowing really hard and drops of rain were hurled at us like bullets shot from the muzzle of a barking machine-gun. We were almost startled by the smooth water found when once the far-outjutting mass of shingle was left safely astern. For a few moments the temptation was almost irresistible to shoot up into the E. road, and to rest for a few hours our wet and chilly bodies, but the fair wind speedily overbore the alluring temptation. Fair winds are not sent to be lightly wasted; the waste of one is almost sure to be followed by bitter regret. With grim determination we kept the yacht to her course.

In the early morning the N. Foreland was abeam, and a course was shaped to round the Longnose buoy and pass up one of the channels that lead to the Thames. This was a foolish decision. Outside the Kentish Knock and round the Long Sand was, on every account, the better route to be taken. But we hoped to carry the flood so far, at least, as the Girdler lightship and, once round the Mouse, to enjoy the benefit of a racing ebb to hurry us to Harwich or on to the Deben. Just before the coming of dawn, close hauled upon the port tack, the yacht was a little above the Prince's Channel lightship. This lightship, then moored at the convergence of the Alexandra and Prince's channels, has long disappeared from the chart of the Thames. The wind was, at the moment, somewhat lighter and had drawn ahead a couple of points. The man who, with any W. in the wind, hopes for a lead up the Thames is more often than not the victim of disappointment. The sea was heavy and in the pitch darkness impossible of evasion. It was of the steep and hollow variety for which, when the wind is meeting the tide, the Thames estuary has won for itself a world-wide notoriety. The flood-tide was nearly done. Anxious to avail ourselves of its assistance as far as was possible, we determined, in the hope of increasing the yacht's speed to re-set the staysail.

The mate, a brother, crawled forward, found the halyard, and, ensuring his safety by seating himself on the deck, gave to the wind the extra canvas. I had just trimmed the sheet, and the mate was still seated forward coiling down the halyard, when the effect of the increased sail was at once disclosed. The yacht was felt to climb a big sea and to poise giddily for a second upon its summit. No doubt could be entertained of what was about to follow. There was but time to yell a warning: "Look out—hang on!" when the yacht dropped down the slope at sickening speed and buried herself recklessly in the next steep surge. It was too dark to see clearly all that actually happened, but the sea thundered on board to the foot of the mast. Cascades of water swept the decks and poured out over the taffrail.

"Are you there forward?" I shouted in the deepest anxiety.

"Aye, I'm here all right, soaked to the skin and full of salt water—but the bowsprit is gone! I can see it alongside under our lee."

"Good Lord! Here's a kettle of fish!"

In the grey of the early dawn while the rain poured down upon our backs, and the wind hummed through the weather shrouds, in a waste of tossing waters, on empty stomachs, we tried our prentice hands on the task of lifting the

spar to our heaving deck. It looked easy enough
to do, but in our inexperience, we found it uncommonly difficult in the doing. The jib was
first unhooked and shoved away below. Then,
risking the far from improbable chance of a
sudden slip overboard, we essayed, with little
success, an attempt to man-handle the ponderous
spar. But every time we had it firmly in our
grasp a heavy lurch either jerked it free of our
hands or caused us to let it go hastily to save our
more precious selves. At last, by running a line
round the butt end, and by hauling on the
bobstay forward, we gained sufficient purchase
to lift it clear of the water and gradually to
manœuvre it along the deck inside the starboard
rigging. We lashed it and its tackle clear of the
staysail sheets and, in a somewhat exhausted
condition, wondered what was next to be done.

Long before the clearance was finished, the ebb
had come strongly down. Almost a dead beat lay
between us and the Girdler lightship. We were by
no means fully assured of the possibility of working
the yacht to windward under her present short
canvas. On trial, however, we found that,
relieved of the weight of the bowsprit, she was
disdainful of the hollow sea and that, though she
showed considerable deliberation in her movements, she never failed to come about in obedience
to the call of the tiller. Six hours were spent in
working over the ebb far enough to windward to

weather the Mouse. Then, with wind aft once more and of much lighter weight, we shook out the reefs, set the topsail, and ran contentedly down the Swin against the flood-tide. The rain ceased and the sun came out to increase our spirits. The kettle was put on and breakfast cooked. It was only 10 a.m., but, after what seemed to be a full day's fight, we felt that the meal might be named, more appropriately, tea. The ebb had already begun when the Deben was reached, but we succeeded in crawling over the bar and in making our way into the river far enough to secure a safe anchorage.

Our mishap roused much sympathy among the good folk ashore, but solely on the ground of expense. "Don't 'ee worrit, master," said Tom Newson, "don't 'ee worrit about it nothin'! You ain't the fust to lose a blame' ow'd bowsprit an' you 'ont be the last neyther, not by a long chalk you 'ont!"

The following summer, within a fortnight, we lost two.

V

ONE BYGONE AUGUST

I

"The splendour of fine bows which yet could stand
The shock of rollers never checked by land.
That art of masts, sail-crowded, fit to break,
Yet stayed to strength, and back-stayed into rake—
The life demanded by that art, the keen
Eye-puckered, hard-case seamen, silent, lean,
They are grander things than all the art of towns,
Their tests are tempests and the sea that drowns."

MASEFIELD.

SO many accounts of trips up and down
Channel have been already published that
it is extremely doubtful whether another will make
the smallest appeal to the most voracious reader
of sea wanderings. There is, however, this to be
said. It matters not how often the same expanse
of water be covered, one may be quite sure that,
on each occasion, circumstances and incidents
will differ entirely from any that have been
before experienced. The contrariety of the unexpected is not the least of the many charms of
cruising. In 1893, still slaves held fast in bondage
by the spell of the S. coast, and hardly, as yet,

aware of the practicability of deep-sea voyaging, we made Scilly the goal to be struggled for. Rouse, who had never been near these outposts of our land, was anxious to view their rocky coasts and to make personal acquaintance with their elusive attraction.

We foregathered on the jetty at Woodbridge in the late afternoon of Thursday, 27th July, Rouse, the boy, and myself. Since 1893, many moons have waxed and waned in the heavens, many tides have ebbed and flowed, not only on the waters, but in the affairs of men. Motor cars were then in their infancy—a tiresome infancy!— marine engines were worked by steam, aeroplanes unthought of, and wireless telegraphy still hidden in the womb of the future. Ships still sailed the seas, though the date of their doom was close at hand. Life was less feverish, and an almost negligible income-tax enabled the poor man to face the upkeep of a yacht without the apprehension and searching of heart that the possession of one too often causes an owner nowadays.

The 6-ton *Senorita* was at her best, her skipper was in his prime, and Rouse, lately established in the post of mate, had scarcely overstepped the watershed that divides youth from manhood. The boy, a youngster of thirteen, was the most excited, if not the happiest, boy in the United Kingdom. An ingenuous youth, absolutely ignorant of the sea, he anticipated upon the rolling

deep a life of unbroken delight, entirely devoid
of distress from wind and wet and *mal-de-mer*.
He fulfilled, so far as it is possible to fulfil, the
rhapsody of the unctuous Mr. Chadband:

> "O running stream of sparkling joy
> To be a soaring human boy."

The yacht lay off the jetty ready for sea with
canvas bent and water on board. The brothers,
John and Harry Moore, old friends rather than
hired servants, lent a hand to stow away our
stack of stores, and at 8 p.m., when there was
sufficient water in the channel to float the boat,
we weighed the anchor and headed down the
river. The northerly breeze of the day had sunk
to a perfect calm, but, by dint of towing and
poling, we made a laborious progress against the
flood to Kison hole, which is the highest anchorage
in the river where vessels of 6 feet draught may
lie afloat. Here we brought up for the night.
The Deben is not a river to be lightly traversed
in the dark. John, a shell-back of long coastal
experience, congratulated us upon the fortune of
breaking out our anchor before the dawn of
Friday. "You ain't come far—that's true enow!
—but you hev' made a start. Beginnin' a vy'ge on
a Friday never done no good to nobody!" They
rowed away in the gathering gloom, leaving us
to complete the safe imprisonment of mobile
goods and chattels, an essential duty on every
sea-going vessel. The boy enlivened our prepara-

tions for turning in. Unacquainted with the art of slipping into a cot, he hit the deck above a resounding rap with his head. The planks rattled, but his brains remained undisturbed. Our commiseration was wasted; he had a skull of marble.

At 3 a.m. the next morning, although there was not a breath of wind, we stowed away our Berthon dinghy, set the canvas, and weighed our anchors. At Kison the river makes a right-angled bend, and the swift ebb, taking charge, swept the yacht forthwith upon the western mud, but, greatly to our relief, we succeeded in shoving clear, and, a light N. breeze arising, were soon speeding down the narrow river. The upper reaches of the Deben, sparsely marked by stakes topped with bunches of brushwood, are, till the water has shot the surrounding flats, almost impossible for an exploring stranger, however experienced he may be in the art of ditch-crawling and in the penetration of puzzling passages.

No poet has ever sung the praises of the Deben, upon its banks are found few beauty spots, no visitors will discover about its waters any distinctive charm, but to the writer personally it will ever remain the river of rivers, for upon its kindly bosom were spent the happiest hours of a lawless boyhood, and every beacon, every reach, every spit recalls some occurrence fit to chill

the blood or excite to laughter. All too late man
recognizes the happiness of youth:

> "When all the world is young, lad,
>   And all the trees are green,
>   And every goose a swan, lad,
>   And every lass a queen."
>
>   KINGSLEY.

and, at least in my own case, everything that will
float, from a dug-out to a sailing-dinghy, an
object of intense desire.

The ebb tide failed before Ramsholt dock was
reached, but the wind was brisk enough to force
the yacht over the growing flood and carry her
out over the bar of the river at 7.45 a.m. She was
headed to cross the Swin and pass through the gut
that leads between the Shipwash and Long Sand
to the Kentish Knock. The passage is well buoyed
and lighted and its only difficulty in clear weather
is due to athwart-running tides which vary in
force from hour to hour. But while I am happier
in threading a way between sands than in in-
vestigating channels beset with rock and reef,
and familiarity breeds a measure of confidence in
the faintest heart, I am fain to admit that the
traversing of these shoal-infested waters always
produces a fine growth of anxiety and that, the
freedom of the open sea safely attained, I conde-
scend to exultant squawking like a bird that has
once more escaped from the net or snare of the
fowler.

The weather was perfectly clear to-day, but the wind gradually headed the yacht. From the Long Sand Head bell-buoy, passed at 1.30 p.m., we had a dead beat up to the lightship on the Kentish Knock. Aided by the returning flood we made the lightship at 6.30 p.m., and gladly let the yacht go off S.W. on her course to the N. Foreland. We were barely at sea before the boy quietly retired to his cot. He stubbornly attributed his uneasiness to early rising and meals at unusual hours. Sea-sick? Of course not! Why should he be? But he was manifestly troubled by the scant sympathy shown by his hard-hearted companions.

In good time I betook myself to the unpleasant but necessary, duty of getting the side-lights ready for the night! An opportunity has been given me recently to read again the *Cruise of the Kate* by Middleton, and the *Voyage Alone in the Yawl Rob Roy*, by McGregor. What surprised me most in both books is the frank admission of the authors that their safety during the hours of darkness depended solely upon a lantern slung in any portion of the rigging convenient at the moment. Efficient lights at sea are of such supreme importance that I have never surrendered their care to another's hands, but have made myself responsible for their daily cleaning and trimming, repulsive and dirty though the work too often proves.

Modern wind-proof lamps, fed with paraffin,

are satisfactory in use and easy to manage, but in 1893 they had either not been invented or had not fallen beneath my cognizance. Their prototypes were an unfailing source of woe and weariness, and might most of them be relied upon to pop out at the very moment when their services were most required. The yacht at the time carried side-lights that burned cera wax, an illuminant of which the late Mr. Macmullen in the account of his 1890 cruise speaks with some enthusiasm. Cera was certainly an improvement upon the colza oil in ordinary use, but it entailed a lot of work, and in cold weather was difficult to ignite. Still, once ignited, it burned without attention, and did away with the need of regular withdrawal from the rigging for clearing away the char and pricking up the wick. Moreover, cera wax was clean to handle, whereas colza oil is a fluid of viscous offensiveness. By the time the lamps were ready I was as seasick as the boy. He hailed with huge delight the discovery of a fellow-sufferer, and waited impatiently for Rouse to succumb to the throes of our common malady. But Rouse remained unaffected by the motion, and jeered at both with a callous lack of fellow-feeling.

The breeze, while steady and of pleasant strength, worked gradually to W.S.W., dead in our teeth. At midnight the light on the N. Foreland winked far to windward on our starboard quarter, and the N. Goodwin flashed in the distance over the end of the bowsprit. Near the Gull lightship, at 6.30 a.m., we put the yacht upon the port tack, and held on till we made the land some little way W. of Deal pier. The Downs were void of shipping, and not a single lugger was in sight afloat. The mild rays of the morning sun lent a counterfeit air of glamour to the long stretch of shingle, the commonplace town and Walmer Castle but giving small play to æsthetic sensibilities, we seized the opportunity of smooth water to make an early breakfast. The boy surprised us by the excellence of his appetite. He ate with voracity, but no lasting benefit. We had, incautiously, told him that food was the best remedy for sea-sickness, and had reason throughout the whole cruise to regret our incautious words. The amount of provisions wasted upon him was enormous.

At 8 a.m., with wind S.W., we were off the S. Foreland, and before the help of the tide was lost, had weathered the Admiralty Pier. By making short boards close along the land we continued to gain ground. Though the coastal scenery is very fine, the narrow waters of the Straits of Dover afford me little pleasure, and I am always glad to leave astern their seething tides and sloppy seas. Several rain squalls induced a hope of a coming shift of wind, and at 3.30 p.m., when Folkestone was abeam, it flew suddenly to W.N.W. The evening came in damp and gloomy·

At dark, the light on Dungeness shone out far to windward. At midnight the yacht was heading towards the land to meet the N.W. breeze of whose coming we felt confident.

In the early hours of Sunday, 30th July, the expected breeze arrived, and by 3 a.m. the yacht was passing Hastings. The water was quite smooth, but the puffs came off the land with such weight that to refrain from reefing demanded a stout heart, but, as each puff was followed by a lull, we carried on, determined to take full advantage of a favouring slant at the cost of what would probably prove only a brief period of discomfort. When Rouse relieved me at 5 a.m., there was a disconsolate look in his sleepy eyes, which disappeared abruptly at the unexpected sight of Beachy Head displaying its gleaming whiteness only a short distance ahead.

At 7 a.m. the yacht was off Newhaven, but far away from the land. Coming up astern was spied a topsail schooner with every yard of canvas spread. We decided that she was a one-time yacht converted into a training ship. She maintained her way down Channel; we made a board inshore. Thereafter, for the greater part of the day, we sailed the yacht on the starboard tack, sometimes on our course for the Owers lightship, generally a shade to southward of it. The weather was beautiful, and the sea was smooth, but sufficiently disturbed to prevent the boy's infirm

7

stomach from recovering a healthy eqilibrium. The wind, hovering between W.N.W. and N.N.W., was of suitable strength, and, though we should have preferred it a point or two more free, we admitted that we had little cause for grumbling, and were hopeful of making the Wight before the day was done, and, before many hours had sped, the tight pinch was recognised as only a blessing in disguise, for the yacht gradually edged away into the track of the homeward-bounders.

In 1868, sitting upon the beach at Aldeburgh, I had the luck to gaze upon a sight which no lapse of time will obliterate from the pages of my memory. After a long spell of S.W. winds there had come a sudden change which brought round the end of Sizewell Bank the vanguard of a huge fleet of sailing craft of every sort and size and rig. Soon the whole bay was crowded by hundreds of vessels making the most of a N. breeze, and the procession showed no sign of diminishing numbers, when, with barely time to catch an evening train, I tore myself reluctantly away. The majority were, no doubt, only humble coasters from the northern coaling ports, but the outer fringe was composed of vessels of the largest size bound to ports at the utmost ends of the world. The panorama formed a spectacle upon which, grown to man's estate, I frequently looked back with unfading interest, but never expected to be in a position to view its like again.

But one never knows what the future has in store. This afternoon for our edification most of the big ships in existence came racing by singly and in clumps of threes and fours, brought in a crowd from the chops of the Channel by a change of wind. For hours our eyes were fascinated by the sight of clipper ships and barques, with every stitch of canvas set and drawing, bending only slightly beneath the breeze that blew steadily upon their quarters. Gipsies of the Horn, manned by hard-bitten crews and commanded by officers even more hard-bitten still, they hurried on to finish off their voyage and land their varied cargoes in the docks of London Town, fated in many cases (the power to bring profit to their owners lost), to pass into the hands of foreigners or, even worse, to end their days in ignominious service. The relentless march of science may not be arrested, but one cannot but lament the passing of the most beautiful structure ever fabricated by the hand of man. With the disappearance of the sailing ship, disappeared as well the greater half of the sea's romance.

Though it was difficult to tear our gaze from the passing pageant, we kept a weather eye open to find the Owers lightship, and, at 5 p.m., sighted it at a distance of several miles to windward. We made a board towards it. After the yacht had been put once more on the starboard tack, the wind blew up freshly, and the sea grew troublesome. Though we headed W., the constant buffeting and adverse tide checked our speed and shattered completely the hope of making the Wight before darkness fell. At 7 p.m. the whippers-in of the passing fleet appeared. Two ships and a barque went closely through our lee and formed a magnificent finale to the grand show of the afternoon. The breeze, which suited them, was too strong for the yacht, and, at dusk, we lay-to and snugged her down. Till midnight we dodged on quietly enough to allow the man below to enjoy some rest.

In the early hours of Monday, 31st July, the glare of St. Catherine's light was visible on the sky behind the intervening land. The yacht's head fell off to S.W. and the outline of Dunnose was recognizable upon the starboard bow. We put about and soon picked up the Nab. The tide was pouring against us, but sheltered by the island we enjoyed smoother water and our pace improved. At 5 a.m., the Warner lightship was close aboard. Coming up astern was the topsail schooner which we had sighted yesterday abreast of Newhaven. We were pleased to find that in the fight to windward she had done no better than ourselves. Thanks to the foul tide racing out of Spithead it was 8 a.m. before we let the anchor go off Wootton creek.

As the boy had kept down no food for about three days, we were seriously concerned about his welfare, and, after a few hours' sleep, hurried him ashore to the little inn at Fishbourne. On his way up from the dinghy he tumbled about like a drunken man, but, regaled on cake and lemonade, he recovered his strength, and was able to walk to Ryde without obvious signs of weakness. A meat tea ashore and a quiet night on board, completed the cure, and he enjoyed life till the yacht was again at sea. Like most sufferers from his distressing malady he insisted upon attributing it to biliousness, the smell of paraffin, the stuffiness of the cabin, to anything, in fact, rather than the rightful cause.

II

"I cannot tell how the truth may be;
I say the tale as 'twas said to me."

SCOTT.

The wind set in strong from S.W. and detained the yacht for several days in the waters about the Wight. Several times we saw at close quarters the *Britannia* racing with the *Meteor, Valkyrie, Satanita, Navahoe*, and were near enough on one occasion to recognize with the naked eye the Duke of York and the German Emperor upon their respective vessels. The boy was greatly disappointed by their appearance. He thought that royalty ought to be distinguished by some conspicuous mark of the divinity that doth hedge a king.

For three days we lay in Swanage bay sheltering from a W. gale, but at 3 a.m. on Saturday,
5th August, weary of inaction, we slipped away,
determined, if it were in any way possible, to
work onwards, at least as far as Portland. The
wind was W.N.W., at the moment moderate, but,
though the bar. was rising, the sky was far from
promising, and we set forth by no means confident
of the accomplishment of our design. On rounding Peveril Ledge buoy we found the sea heavy,
but, with the wind blowing slightly off the land,
we dashed and plunged as far as Anvil head in a
most exhilarating fashion. Then, all shelter lost,
without wasting a moment upon deliberation,
we hauled the staysail a-weather, put two reefs in
the mainsail, and took the staysail off. Half the
wet coil of the latter's halyard went up out of
reach, and, so violent was the motion of the
yacht, that the clamber aloft to recover the end
proved a singularly unpleasant task. The shelter
of the cockpit was scarcely gained before a sea
pitched over the bows, and removed the in-
securely fastened fo'c's'le hatch. It was, fortunately, captured before it reached the water, and
tightly battened down by the time another sea
landed on the fore deck.

The tide, pouring westward, shoved us to windward fast. Some distance S.W. of St. Alban's
head the yacht was tacked and headed to pass
through the Race, not without a shadow of anxiety

on our part, for, in those days, we felt for this area of tumbling water a respect which has been completely destroyed by longer experience. St. Alban's Race shows plenty of flurry and fuss, but is remarkably free from dangerous vice. On the port tack, with sea nearly abeam, we crossed without the smallest trouble, and eventually made the land a short distance W. of Kimmeridge Ledge. Soon the wind fell lighter, and it was noon before we brought up in the S.W. corner of Portland harbour. The cabin was a regular hurrah's nest, its floor littered with the boy's collars, handkerchiefs, and underclothing, lying cheek by jowl with the frying-pan and other utensils of our culinary outfit.

As soon as the anchor was down the wind came away from N., and several coasters seized the chance of getting away to the westward, but, keen as we were not to allow a fair wind to blow to waste, we felt that we deserved a rest after a hard and soaking hammer to windward, and were not tempted to move.

At the N. end of the Portland peninsula lies the hamlet of Castleton. It possesses, now, quays and landing steps, but, in those far-off days— unless, indeed, my memory is hopelessly astray— nothing of the kind existed. In the evening we landed on a flat and rugged beach where a gently inebriated longshoreman assisted us to carry the dinghy above high-water mark, and, that service ended, led us without a word to the nearest public-house. Presumably we wore the look of thirsty souls. Requested to name his drink, the man chose cider, declaring that to be the only refreshment that he ever took. After a stroll through Chesilton to Fortune's Well we turned upon our tracks and, assisted by the same man now very unsteady on his legs, we launched the boat and gained the yacht. Imagining it to be a temperance drink, we had regaled the boy on cider, but, after the late demonstration of its intoxicating power, we assured him with becoming gravity that in future his thirst must be assuaged by some less potent fluid. We were determined to avoid the reproach of being the first to put his feet upon the downward track that led to inebriety. Portland, it appeared, had proved a terrible disappointment. He had confidently anticipated the sight of desperate convicts making wild dashes for liberty and hotly pursued by determined warders armed to the teeth and using their weapons.

The following morning, Sunday, 6th August, turning out at 5 a.m. we made an immediate start with a light N.N.E. wind, a rising bar. and every appearance of settled weather. The wind promptly died away, and an hour passed before the yacht slipped through the S. entrance of the harbour, now blocked by a sunken vessel. The strong tide setting upon the land forced a smack

and a brig ahead to let their anchors go in haste.
The yacht was put upon the starboard tack, and,
assisted by a small S.E. breeze, soon drew off the
land sufficiently to allow her to weather the E.
corner of the peninsula. At 9 a.m. the Bill was
abeam. The breeze lasted just long enough to
carry us past, and then veered too far to S. to
allow the setting of the spinnaker which we
were in the act of withdrawing from its bag.
Portland Race is, undeniably, peculiarly nasty,
and exacts respect from every cruiser who has
been near enough to view its violence or
listen to its roar. The passage inside along
the land always fills my heart with nervous
apprehension lest a wrongly calculated tide
should force the helpless yacht into the middle
of the turmoil.

The morning, bright and clear, permitted an
unusually fine view of the distant coast, but,
later, clouds obscured the sky, some rain fell, and
the wind went so far W. that, when at 2.30 p.m.
Berry head was sighted, the yacht was pointing
no higher up than Dartmouth. A determination
to spend the night in harbour was altered by the
freeing of the wind, and we decided that, if
possible, Falmouth should be our next port of
call. At 8 p.m. the Start was weathered. We were
anxious to change the big for a smaller jib before
the fall of darkness. The heavy sea off the Start
advised postponement of the work. The big jib,

at all times a troublesome sail, was almost dangerous at night. Off Prawle point, though the sea was not appreciably less, the desired exchange was safely made. The boy, forgetting for the moment the nausea which had laid him low for hours, stood in the cockpit, with flushed cheeks and shining eyes, ready to hurl an uplifted life-buoy if his skipper lost his foothold and tumbled overboard. It was impossible to decide whether he was the more relieved or disappointed by my return aft from activities on the fore deck. He wished me no harm, but, apparently, felt that high excitement deserved a less lame and impotent conclusion.

With wind abeam the yacht was steered W. by N. In time the light on the Eddystone was picked up ahead. The wind fell faint and fog came down. At 5 a.m., without a breath of wind, we were close to the invisible Eddystone. At 7 a.m., during a momentary break in the fog, the lighthouse was descried directly over the stern. We must have drifted very closely past. Weary waiting was, eventually, ended by a little S.S.E. breeze, which carried the yacht but slowly against the now E. running stream. The fog cleared off the sea, but continued to conceal the land. At noon the outline of the Dodman showed up vaguely on our beam, but it was 3.30 p.m. before we managed to drag slowly past the lighthouse on St. Anthony. Finding a better breeze inside, we worked up the harbour quickly, and half an hour later brought up in a comfortable berth under the shelter of the town.

The buildings that line the waterside are quaintly irregular and the narrow streets arouse a temporary interest in a stranger's eyes, but Falmouth harbour, or rather, perhaps, the estuary of the Fal, deserves every epithet of appreciation that has ever been bestowed upon it. The man who delights in sheltered sailing can find fresh waters to explore for many days in succession. But the glory of the roads is unfortunately departed. In bygone times they were ever crowded with the finest examples of naval architecture and the rigger's art; now they lie open, clear of anchored shipping, mournfully desolate. Falmouth has ceased to be a port of call. No sailing craft are left, and to the steamboat wireless telegraphy transmits the necessary orders. A pilot cutter still hangs about between St. Anthony and the Lizard, but weeks must often elapse without bringing a job to cheer the hearts of its patient occupants.

Here several pleasant but uneventful days were spent. The boy enjoyed the easy life and smooth water, and, ignoring his previous sickliness, assumed the airs of a confident and hardy mariner. In fact, to use the figurative words of Scripture, he waxed fat and kicked! The only excitement of our stay was provided by the

Two Brothers, a light barge, which beating down the harbour against a S.E. wind under the management of a single hand, was, incautiously, entangled amid a crowd of anchored yachts. Inside of all she was put about. A moment's observation showed that, with the leeway she was making, she had not the faintest chance of weathering the *Senorita*. The helmsman tried to tack again, but the barge came into the wind, hung hesitating, and then began to drive steadily in our direction. Letting the jib sheet fly and throwing its halyard off the cleat, the man dropped the anchor in the hope of checking in time his charge's drift. We on our part slacked away fathom after fathom of chain in frantic haste to avoid, if possible, the threatened blow. All efforts were vain. The barge soon bumped into the yacht, fortunately almost broadside to broadside and without doing apparent damage, but our bowsprit, piercing the slatting jib, pinned the vessels together in a close and un-desired embrace.

Help came from neighbouring yachts. By hauling on a rope made fast about our mast the pressure forward was relieved sufficiently to allow the jib to be cleared, and, the bond re-moved, the vessels swung apart. Our topmast was fortunately, housed, and the only evidence left of the late collision was the barge's ruined sail. The boy was wildly excited. A real adventure at last! He disapproved most strongly of the bestowal upon our helpers of spirituous refreshment. That obligation, surely, ought to be met by the ship at fault! His sense of justice was shockingly outraged.

On Friday, 11th August, with wind S.S.W. and weather dull, we put forth to work to Penzance, a port as yet unvisited. At 0.45 p.m. off the Lizard we met the steamboat *Navarro* towing the disabled *Wandle*. The sea off the point was heavy, but, bearing away N.W. by W., we felt it but little, and, when later the yacht was headed N.W.$\frac{1}{2}$W. direct for Penzance, we felt it even less. The run across Mount's Bay was entirely pleasant. At 4.15 p.m. we shot the piers and were soon comfortably berthed in an almost empty dock. In the evening, after a half-hearted exploration of the town, we invaded the smoking-room of the Queen's hotel to rest our legs and quench our thirst. It had taken no long experience to discover that the climate of Penzance induced lassitude and a longing for cooling draughts. While we lingered over our refreshment and watched through the open window the movements on the parade outside, an elderly gentleman, the only other occupant of the room, entered in conversation about yachts and yachting, and, in the end, told us the following tale.

Many years ago, in the days of his early manhood, he was eager to board a certain troopship, bringing home from India a regiment of soldiers, in order to secure a contract for the supply of beer to the canteen. He was a brewer, and in keen competition with a rival brewer, named Brooke, to be first on board this particular ship. Brooke owned a small yacht, the narrator chartered a Portsmouth boat owned by two brothers of the name of Baker. One afternoon, tired of hard sitting and of hope deferred, they returned to Portsmouth to lay in provisions and enjoy a few hours of rest. Our friend had just laid him lown to sleep when Bill Baker rushed to his hotel to say that the vessel's arrival off the Lizard had been telegraphed and that Brooke, having renewed supplies, was in the act of setting forth again.

"Then we'll lay in provisions and be off ourselves. All that night we lay between the Warner and the Nab. At daylight we saw Brooke's boat lying at anchor under Bembridge. We set our canvas, but the faint air soon died away and we betook ourselves to rowing. The sound of the oars roused Brooke's crew. They made sail, and feeling a breeze off the land which failed to reach our canvas, they speedily left us helpless far astern. Tide alone carried us as far as Ventnor. Bill Baker said, 'Well, mister, he's too good for us, and there's only one way that I can see of fore-reaching out to windward. Let's go ashore here, strip the boat of masts and sails so she shan't be recognized, lie on our bellies on the cliff and watch. If he goes right away down channel, we're completely done; if he ups helm, as I 'spects he will, to save tide back to his old anchorage, we'll win the weather-gage and keep it, too, I reckon.'

"So ashore we went, disguised the boat and clambered to the top of the cliffs. We had not been lying long before Baker cried, 'There, what did I tell you? He has put his helm up and, if so be he don't spy our boat, he'll slip back to Bembridge for the night.' We watched him pass. After some breakfast I chartered a trap and drove along till we were near enough to see Brooke's yacht at anchor in her previous berth. That evening we started away again and next morning picked up the trooper. Satisfactory arrangements were made with the colonel and, before that regiment went abroad again, it must have paid me £18,000, or even more. Several hours after the business had all been settled, Brooke fell in with the ship and was put on board in the yacht's dinghy. You can imagine how crestfallen he looked when he saw his rival comfortably installed upon the quarter-deck." With regard to this yarn I would call the reader's attention to the lines of Scott quoted at the head of the chapter.

On leaving the hotel the boy decided that a brewer's life was the life for him, and that his share of the business should be confined to the exciting duty of waylaying troopers to make lucrative contracts for the alleviation of the thirst of sun-baked soldiers.

The following morning, in a fog thick enough to wet like rain, we joined the passengers on Warren's coach to be driven to the Logan Stone and austere Land's End. The sun came out and the day turned oppressively hot. Consequently, at the first halt, it was a very languid company that trudged across some fields to view the Logan Stone, and refused to succumb to the guide's enthusiasm when the object of their search was reached. An ill-advised naval officer is said, with the help of a body of bluejackets, to have heaved the stone over the cliffs. Bidden by the authorities to restore it to its pedestal, he succeeded in obeying orders only at the cost of his fortune. The stone, though replaced exactly, has lost most of its old-time mobility.

In due time we reached the scattered hamlet that in those days crowned the extremity of Land's End. Several houses bore on one side the legend "The last house in England," and on the other "The first house in England." In each case presumably the legend once was true, but a fresh interloper erected nearer to the edge of the cliff has robbed each in turn of an empty honour.

Fog still hung heavily over sea and coast, and hid from our eyes the grim outline of the cliffs.

"Senorita" : THE REACHING JIB

After lunch at one of the many restaurants we dozed away the time till the hour fixed for our return. The air was absolutely still and oppressive with muggy heat. On disembarking at Penzance we strolled off wearily towards the dock. On the way a most amusing sight caused us to forget for a moment our tired legs and the clamminess of our environment.

In front of us strode two fishermen, each equipped with a jug, and evidently bent upon the purchase of the supper beer. One of them suddenly lashed out an arm in pursuit of a fly. His raid was successful, and, boasting of his success, he carefully opened his closed fist, just enough to disclose to his companion the imprisoned captive. Unexpectedly, with a startled exclamation, he opened his fist wide, and the supposed fly escaped. "Christ!" he cried, "it's a ruddy bee! Stung me solid it has too! Who'd ha' thought it!" Loud was the laughter of a knot of spectators. Any instance of *captor captus* is sure to arouse derision.

On Monday, 14th August, at 6 a.m., we hauled out of the basin with a faint S.W. draught, which carried the yacht clear of the piers and the Gear rock, and then, utterly exhausted, fell into the deepest sleep. Till 5 p.m. we sweltered in muggy heat, lollopping about in the middle of a fleet of luggers out of Newlyn, which had drifted into our neighbourhood and rolled about as helplessly

8

as the yacht, much too near to be regarded with absolute indifference. At last a schooner was spied in the distance, running W. with an E. breeze. In time, the same wind reached the yacht, which, besides setting her in motion, lifted from the hearts of her crew a heavy cloud of irritation. Later, we had much difficulty in avoiding the long lengths of drift nets put into the water by the luggers, but before dark we had worked out clear, and, with the Wolf Rock light gleaming on the port bow, were on our course for Scilly.

We enjoyed a lovely night. The wind a trifle S. of E. blew steadily and allowed the yacht to run her course W.$\frac{1}{4}$N. without much danger of gybing. By midnight the lights on St. Agnes and Round Island lighted our road with dazzling brilliance. Soon after 3 a.m. we were close to the islands, and prudently lay to to wait for daylight. The tide carried the yacht rapidly northward, but in the early dawn we reached along the coast of St. Mary, and, gybing round Peninnis head, were brought up before 6 a.m. off Hugh Town in St. Mary's Pool. The boy, awakened by the rattle of the escaping chain, thrust out a sleepy head and gazed around with lacklustre eye. He declined to believe that the yacht had reached Scilly. The islands, he thought, were much too big. Informed that the place ashore was Hugh Town, he cried in triumph:

"I knew it wasn't Scilly—trying to pull my leg again!—but you can't take me in this time—so there!"

III

"Hurrah for the homeward bound!"
GILBERT.

The Scilly Islands are too well known to demand description. "Only in calm weather and in broad daylight can the boatman who knows the place venture in these waters. Not even the most skilled boatman would steer for the outer islands at sunset. For there are hidden rocks, long ridges of teeth that run out from the islands, to tear and grind to powder any boat that should be caught in their devouring jaws. There are currents, also, which run swiftly and unexpectedly between the islands, to sweep the boat along with them till it shall strike the rocks and go down with any who are aboard! and there are strong gusts which sweep round the headlands and blow through the narrow sounds." So Mr. Besant in *Armorel of Lyonesse*. Despite his lurid account excursions may be safely made by daylight between most of the islands about the time of high tide, for then the visible dangers are easily avoided, and the hidden ones are buried beneath a comfortable 12 feet of water.

The days of our stay were marked by abnormally quiet weather. One breathless afternoon, in reckless mood, we rowed in the Berthon dinghy across the roads, and, landing on Sampson, endeavoured to decide which of the ruined cottages had been the home of Armorel. The book had been published only a year or two before. Though we were unable to satisfy ourselves about which of the cottages the author had in mind, we enjoyed his lucid exposition of the outlying islands. The remains of the cottages showed that Sampson had once been inhabited, but the only living creatures we saw upon it were a few cows and quantities of black rabbits. The calm, fortunately, continued, and we regained the yacht with ease. But it was a rash adventure, which might well have ended in the marooning of the adventurers.

Two days sufficed to exhaust the attractions of the islands, and, on Thursday, 17th August, we started upon our homeward voyage. Lack of wind detained us at our anchorage all the morning, but at 3 p.m., with a gentle breathing from S. by E., we weathered Peninnis head, and put the yacht upon her course E. by S.$\frac{1}{2}$S. to make the Lizard. The wind freshened but drew well ahead, the sea grew big enough to deaden the yacht's way, and it was 8.30 p.m. before we neared the land with the Longships light open on the starboard bow. On the port tack, with water smooth and a fresh breeze off the land, we raced close past the Longships towards the alternating gleams of red and white flashed from the Wolf Rock lighthouse, and the yacht, shoved to windward by a mighty tide, was, at midnight, well to the eastward of this insidious danger. The wind worked round so far that soon on the starboard tack we were heading our course to the Lizard.

My sleep below was suddenly disturbed by an animated exchange of invective between Rouse and the skipper of a coasting schooner, which, coming up astern with extinguished side-lights, had nearly succeeded in running the yacht down. Providentially, Rouse heard her wash in time, and warned her off by a hasty display of the binnacle lamp. Just before daylight returned, an approaching steamboat, with her lights all open, showed an unswerving determination to force upon us her undesired acquaintance. The wind was too light to allow escape by flight, the binnacle lamp was out, and I was by no means confident of the brilliance of our side-lights. Half a box of matches, ignited in a bunch, made a sufficient flare to rouse the boat's attention to our presence, and, starboarding her helm, she gave us generous room. One knows from experience that in the hour before dawn is due, when Nature is at its lowest ebb and sleep bears heavy on weary eyes, there is a temptation to be neglectful of safeguards and to take unwarrantable risks. The adventures of the night impressed upon us the widsom of carrying in the cockpit a powerful light ready to be shown, without a moment's delay, to vessels that threaten a too near approach.

The day came out warm and fine with just a pleasant breeze from S.W. The Lizard was abeam soon after 9 a.m. We passed the Dodman at 2.45 p.m., and by 4.15 p.m. were comfortably moored in Fowey harbour.

The boy was a clumsy swimmer. With fists tightly clenched he paddled about like a drowning puppy on the rare occasions when he could be persuaded to loosen his grip of the accommodation ladder. This evening, incited by wily flattery and the promise of a shilling, he undertook to swim round the yacht next morning encased for safety in a cumbersome cork jacket. His cupidity was still further whetted by the offer of a reward if he turned out early, and extinguished the riding-light. He went betimes to bed in the greatest glee, counting up with foolish confidence the pecuniary gains of the coming morrow.

But the boy was fated to learn that it is foolish, to quote the lines of Samuel Butler,

> "To swallow gudgeons ere they're catched,
>   And count their chickens ere they're hatched,"

for Rouse, happening to be awake soon after 4 a.m., slipped quietly forward, extinguished the riding-light and brought it below. Three hours later, with yawns and groans, and much bumping of head and elbows, the boy tumbled out of his cot, and pausing a moment to gather courage, dashed forward barefooted over the dew-laden deck. It was a very disgusted boy that returned a moment later to his disordered blankets. He stubbornly refused to attempt the promised swim, and treated us all day with withering contempt. A few days later, off Wootton, he was chaffed into accomplishing the deed he had undertaken, but he clung so closely to the side of the yacht that Rouse was unable to obtain the snapshot with which he hoped to commemorate the occasion. The promised shilling was spent upon unripe plums. "A fool and his money are soon parted," chuckled Rouse. The boy, after long deliberation, retorted: "Not half such a fool as you think! If the plums had been ripe, you would have wanted a share; as they are sour, I shall have the lot to myself!"

By noon we were clear of the harbour bound for Yealm, another port as yet unvisited. The wind was S.W. and strong. At 2.40 p.m. we passed Rame head, and, heading for the Mew-stone, were soon approaching our unknown harbour. The water was low, but we were confronted by no special difficulty. The canvas was taken off as we rounded Misery point and the yacht drove slowly up to a convenient berth. Yealm was still free from the plague of house-

boats which now leave little anchorage open for
the use-of strangers. The inhabitants of Plymouth
have discovered the beauties of his land-locked
pool, and take full advantage of its sylvan
rusticity.

The morning of Monday, 21st August, was wet
and stormy, but later the sun burst through the
clouds, and, though the S.W. wind still blew
strongly, we started at 11.30 a.m., with topmast
housed and a double-reefed mainsail, to run to
Dartmouth.   About noon Yealm head was
rounded, and soon, clear of the land, the yacht
was careering wildly upon her course for Bolt
Tail.   The sea was heavy, but the yacht ran dry,
though one curler popped over the quarter and
wetted the occupants of the cockpit with unexpected thoroughness. At 2.45 p.m. we gybed
round the Start, and, running outside the Skerries,
were in the very entrance of Dartmouth harbour
by 4 p.m. The surroundings of this harbour are
beautiful, but scarcely beautiful enough to
counterbalance the exasperation it usually provides. Headed on every tack by shifting flaws,
we spent an hour and a half in working over the
ebb to an anchorage above the *Britannia*. The
naval college was not yet built, and the old ship
enhanced with a touch of romance the natural
beauty of the river. Our tea was graced by a pot
of Devonshire cream. The boy, introduced for
the first time to this delicacy, partook of it so

freely that he suffered from internal pains the greater part of the night.

The following morning on the last of the ebb, with a S.W. draught, we drifted out to sea, and, on passing the Mewstone at 8 a.m., set a course E.$\frac{1}{2}$S. for Portland Bill. We had a fine passage. The boy soon disappeared below. In spite of his trouble during the night he insisted upon eating his share of the remainder of the cream at breakfast, and stoutly refused to admit that he was now paying the penalty of greed. The wind grew steadily and the sea made. Ordinary prudence bade us reef, but we scorned its dictates. Strong physically and confident of our skill, we were still prone to carry on to the last moment rather than to consult our comfort by a timely shortening of canvas. The immediate result was a very sketchy dinner of potted meat and biscuits.

At 2.30 we had the Portland lights in one. To give the Race a wider berth, the yacht was brought a couple of points nearer to the wind. Thereupon a good deal of the channel flew over the crew and sails. Though well to seaward of the Race, we passed through an area disturbed by irregular and breaking seas, and were uncommonly glad when, the danger past, we were able to bring the yacht back to her course and show her heels to the pursuing foes. With wind and tide together, we were through St. Alban's Race before we

thoroughly realized that we had entered it.
Beyond Swanage the sea proved quieter, and,
with the wind now W., directly aft, we managed
to boil the kettle and make up for a meagre dinner
by a substantial tea. At 7 p.m. we passed the
Needles, eleven hours from Dartmouth Mewstone,
a distance of 80 miles. A glorious run scarcely
marred by its expensiveness! The mast, badly
rung at the hounds, was condemned at the end of
the trip, and a new one ordered for the following
season.

The wind a shade to the N. by W. necessitated
a gybe to run up to Hurst. By scandalizing the
mainsail the manœuvre was safely accomplished.
We carried a drain of tide as far as Yarmouth,
but it was 9.30 p.m. before Cowes was reached.
The Royal Yacht, brilliantly lighted fore and aft,
was evidently entertaining guests. Once round
Old Castle point we found the wind very light,
and crept only slowly towards our proposed
anchorage off Wootton creek. At 11 p.m. the
anchor was let go. Some mulligatawny soup had
long been ready and, after a hasty stowage of the
canvas, we hurried below to consume the savoury
mess. The boy was already asleep, but he roused
up sufficiently to admit that the soup smelled
good. He refused to touch his portion on
the plea that it was made of beastly goose-
skins.

IV

"*Watch*. If we know him to be a thief, shall we not lay
     hands on him?

"*Dogberry*. Truly, by your office, you may; but I think
     they that touch pitch will be defiled; the most peace-
     able way for you, if you do take a thief, is, to let him
     show himself what he is, and steal out of your
     company."

SHAKESPEARE.

Wednesday, 23rd August, was very wet and we
postponed a necessary visit to Ryde for letters till
the rain cleared up in the afternoon. Intending to
be back before nightfall, we neglected to sling
the riding-light to the forestay before leaving for
the shore. But the lethargy engendered by a
square meal and the temptation of a band delayed us at Ryde till dark, and it was after 10 p.m.
when we started from Fishbourne to paddle to
the yacht, pleasantly wearied by unaccustomed
walking and totally unsuspicious of the disagreeable surprise we were shortly to experience.

When, after unlocking the sliding hatch, I
stepped down the ladder into the cabin, my
nostrils were assailed by an unaccountable smell
of spirits. In curiosity rather than alarm, I struck
a hasty match, and by its flickering light sighted
the floor untidily disordered with locker lids.
"By Jingo," I exclaimed, "the yacht has been
broken into and burgled!"

Soon the rays of the lighted lamp showed that

my exclamation was amply justified. The reek of
spirits was explained by the sight of our last
bottle of whisky lying empty with neck knocked
off. Rouse had, inadvertently, left his watch
behind. That was gone. His valuable pocket
barometer had also disappeared. A spirit stove,
the kettle, all our spare pipes were missing. A
wail from the boy announced the loss of his most
cherished treasure, a knife of gigantic size if of
questionable edge. Entrance had been made
through a forced skylight. The burglars, hearing
our approach or otherwise disturbed, had,
evidently, made a hasty departure without time,
fortunately, to make a clean sweep of all our belongings. The atmosphere of the cabin was distinctly sulphurous as we slunk into our cots in a
mood of blind but helpless fury.

As the stolen watch was the only one on board
in working order, the exact hour of our breakfast
cannot be exactly stated. The W. wind was strong,
but, leaving the boy on board with strict in-
junctions to repel all intruders with the boat-hook,
we struggled to the shore, and reported the out-
rage to a sympathetic coastguard. He attributed
the robbery to hooligans from Ryde, and advised
us to apply to the police for help. His half-
hearted advice betrayed a well-founded disbelief in the utility of the application. Rouse
hurried off to the village of Wootton on the
chance of meeting a constable upon his regular

beat, whilst I sped away to Ryde to report the robbery at police headquarters.

At Ryde my tale of woe was heard with a chilling show of indifference. The crime had been committed outside the jurisdiction of the town; the county police were the people before whom the matter must be laid. Following directions given, I trudged a mile or more into the country, growing at every step more hot and dusty and more depressed by a growing sense of the futility of my journey. But with weary legs I continued on my way, and, at length, reached a flower-embowered villa which bore above its door the inscription "County Police." The sergeant was off the premises, but a constable gave me audience and noted down particulars. The interview led to nothing, but had its amusing side.

Informed that a boy was a member of the crew, the constable snapped his notebook to-gether with an air of finality, smacked his lips exultantly, and declared the boy to be the culprit. "Varmints!" he ejaculated, "they boys be at the bottom of every mischief!" Even the fact, apart from other considerations, that the boy was ashore with us when the crime was perpe-trated, failed to shake his belief that he had dis-covered the guilty party. That ended the business; it seemed useless to pursue it further. After pur-chasing at Ryde a cheap clock and a kettle, I returned to the yacht with the hope that the

Almighty would in His good time inflict upon
the thieves an appropriate punishment. Ignorance
of their future, whether they flourished like the
bay tree of the Psalmist or were brought to
justice on another charge, even now rouses in
my vengeful heart a feeling of discontent.

Ashore in the evening to purchase bread at the
inn at Fishbourne, we found the landlady highly
interested in our adventure and indignant about
our losses. She was reminded of an occurrence
that had lately happened within her knowledge.
A man stole a boat. Next he sneaked ashore and
stole a lamb. But he soon suffered for his mis-
deeds, for he was driven ashore somewhere to the
eastward—Langston ways or thereabouts—and
she believed she was right—though she might be
mistaken—the man was still in prison working
out the sentence inflicted for his thieving. "But
what I sez do seem hard—them as loses their
property be no ways better off for the thief's
bein' caught." This struck the boy, too, as being a
shocking defect in our legal system. The State,
he thought, ought to reimburse the victim as well
as punish the criminal.

On 25th August, anxious to quit the scene of
the robbery, we were away by 5.15 a.m. with a
W.S.W. breeze, bound for the Deben or some
adjacent port. The boy, forcibly ejected from his
cot to wind up a fishing-line left over the side, fell
asleep quicker than he wound, and, in the end, we

were obliged to wind it up ourselves. The wind was light, but by 7.30 a.m. we had fetched the Nab lightship, and at 9 a.m. were entering the Looe channel. The tide had already begun to run to the westward, but the wind improved, and half an hour later the Mixon beacon was left astern. With wind dead aft, the yacht was run for Beachy Head.

The day was bright and warm, the wind steady, and water smooth. At 4 p.m. the tide came away in our favour, and at 5.40 p.m. Beachy Head was abeam. For hours we had been in hot pursuit of a barge. Round the head, the wind drawing off the land, we gybed the boom to starboard, and, with the headsails now doing their work, quickly overhauled our rival, the *Lord Beaconsfield*. It is a curious fact that, while many a boat has been called after the Conservative statesman, no owner, within my knowledge, has ever attempted, by using his name, to uphold the fame of Gladstone, his Liberal opponent.

As evening approached, the wind fell lighter, but never absolutely failed. At dusk it breezed up again, and the yacht with strong tide beneath her bottom hurried on past Hastings. At 9 p.m. we were passing Fairlight. The boy carried out a long-expressed intention of keeping a night watch, and joined Rouse in the cockpit when he took charge of the deck, but, having eaten the biscuits and chocolate provided as much to help forward lagging time as to appease incipient hunger, he concluded that he was not interested, and tumbled into his bed. Dungeness was rounded at 11 p.m.

Saturday, 26th August, began with a N. wind that displayed a vigour which caused the topsail to be pulled down and reefing to be considered. Though the water was smooth, the lee rail was constantly awash. The night was bright, with a moon almost full and complete absence of cloud, but the atmosphere was bitterly cold and quite devoid of moisture. At 2.20 a.m. the yacht was half-way between the S. Foreland lights. As soon as the high land was cleared, we came into a breeze blowing from W.N.W. and more moderate in strength. As the tide was now pouring in our teeth we decided to pass through the Downs by running close along the shelving beach.

By 7 a.m. we had negotiated the Old Cudd channel opposite Ramsgate, and were approaching Broadstairs. Breakfast was already under way, for we had prudently done our cooking before the shelter of the land was lost. The boy, roused up to eat, was promptly ill, a misfortune caused, he insisted by insufficient sleep due to the time spent in the cockpit the previous night. The N. Foreland reached, we were called upon to decide whether to run on N.E. to make the Kentish Knock, or, working the tides, to take eht longer route *via* the Thames. For reasons now

forgotten, we determined, if it were possible, to
spend the night in the E. Swale. A curiosity to
investigate the approaches of a strange shelter
was, probably, the chief reason of our decision.
The wind was now N.W., but we hoped that the
flood-tide would last long enough to carry us
round Whitstable Street buoy into the harbour
we wished to visit.

And for a time our hope seemed likely to be
realized. Rounding the Long Nose buoy, we
worked up the coast with encouraging speed.
The wind was of satisfactory strength, and the
tidal sea not conspicuously vicious. But at
11.30 a.m., when the flood was growing slack,
the yacht was only a short distance past the
Reculvers, and the wind, though it had worked
to N.N.W., had fallen very light. Half-way across
Herne bay we met the ebb in strength. Whitstable was in sight, but a long time elapsed before
the Street buoy was picked up. After a short
board off, the wind came a little stronger. We
found and weathered the buoy, and, running up
the Swale came to an anchor at 2.30 p.m. a
little to the West of Shellness point.

The boy, who had spent the day in his cot,
roused by the noise of our bringing up, made his
way to the deck and gazed with undisguised
satisfaction upon what he supposed to be the
yacht's final anchorage. He had, evidently, not
overheard, or had not understood our discussion

about entering the Swale, and was in no doubt but that the trip was over, and that he was at last in a position to recall with present delight the, at the time, doubtful pleasures of his voyage.

"Well, do you know where you are?" he was asked. He replied scornfully:

"Yes, of course I do—the mouth of the Deben!"

"How did you recognize it?"

"By the two trees together, an oak and a poplar, which I happened to notice when we went out of the river."

He was congratulated, with as grave a demeanour as we were able to assume, upon the keenness of his observation. He regarded with a contemplative eye Rouse's occasional fits of hysterical chuckling, and was, evidently, surprised that no preparations were made to pay a visit to the shore, but any rising suspicion that things might not be altogether what they seemed was, eventually, swept away by an unexpected excitement.

At dusk, when we were engaged upon an unhurried meal, there was brought to our ears the sound of a brass band playing "The Lost Chord." A rush was made to the deck to seek an explanation of this mysterious music. A smack dragging a trawl was driving slowly up on the young flood. Her deck was crowded with beanfeasters, to whom a blaring band discoursed music of mediocre sweetness. To the inquiring boy it was

explained that music had charms for even fish
and was often used to tempt them into the fatal
meshes of a net. Why then, was asked, do not all
smacks carry a band? Because the supply of
musicians able to face the sea with complacency,
was exceedingly limited, and, consequently, the
cost of a sea-going band was heavy, too heavy
indeed for the majority of smack-owners to
undertake. That evening, it is to be feared, the
Senorita kept the recording angel busily at work.

In the morning the boy was persuaded that, as
Rouse had still a day to spare, we purposed
spending it at sea. He acquiesced with a sigh, for
he had pictured to himself a happy journey
home and the warm welcome given to a travelled
wanderer. We started at 6 a.m. with the reasonable
expectation of reaching the Deben before dark.
The weather was hazy. Owing partly to haze,
partly to distraction from the tiller by my breakfast egg, I put the yacht just westward of the
Spit buoy, upon the Columbine. The accident
caused delay, but was not, otherwise, of the
smallest importance. The rising tide soon floated
off the yacht. The breeze was good from N.N.W.
Crossing near to the E. Spaniard and Gilman
buoys, we fetched on a close pinch the Girdler
lightship and the E. Oaze buoy, whence a board
or two carried us to windward of the Mouse
lightship.

As we drew near, a man was spied upon her

decks making wild signals to attract attention. "Letters," I murmured. Amid tokens of the wildest delight on the part of the boy, we ran closely by, and a letter ballasted with a biscuit was tossed on board. The boy's excitement was soon explained. He imagined that there were letters for us and him! That by some means they had been conveyed to the lightship to be delivered to the yacht if she happened to pass near enough to receive them. Such innocence was too pathetic to be bantered. He was in no way interested in a letter passed on board simply to be posted. To alleviate his disappointment he was allowed, at his earnest request, to eat the biscuit. But this proved a disappointment, too. After the first mouthful his eagerness to share with us the prize was a conclusive proof that ship's bread met with little approval.

Soon after 11 a.m. with flood-tide running up strongly, the yacht rounded the Maplin light-house. The wind turned shy, but, by borrowing boldly on the Maplin sand, we fetched the Swin Middle lightship without a board. Up to noon the day, though dull and cold, proved reason-ably satisfactory, but the afternoon was diversified by a mixture of calms and N.E. squalls.

Near the Whitaker buoy we felt the ebb which, after we had pushed with difficulty through the Spitway, swept the yacht steadily in the direction of the Naze. When a breeze blew up again, it blew from dead ahead. At 6.30 p.m. we had Harwich abeam, and debated whether to make certain of a port or to risk a night outside by continuing our way to the Deben. The distance yet to be covered was only 7 miles, and, if we failed to save our daylight, we should have the advantage of a bright moon to assist our passage over the bar. We determined to take the risk.

We did not near the entrance till some time after dark, and, brightly as the moon shone, its beams proved a sorry substitute for daylight. We could neither find the buoy nor see our way into the river, and were on the point of bringing up for the night when the lugsail of an approaching boat was happily descried. We readily succumbed to the offer of a pilot, and, running in on the young flood, were by 9.30 p.m. safely moored in the quiet backwater that lies between the Horse sand and the western shore. The boy was greatly surprised at being asked if he did not recognize the place. How could he recognize a place he had never visited? At allusions to oaks and poplar trees he only sighed and looked un utterable things. He did not discover that the yacht had reached home waters till the following morning, when the address on his letters gave away the secret.

But the boy enjoyed the cruise so much, at any rate, in retrospect, that, for many years in succession, he made one of the *Senorita's* crew. The trip was remarkably void of excitement caused by weather. One cannot but think that the Augusts of old were finer than the Augusts of the present day. Statistics would, quite likely, prove that the idea is entirely unfounded. But, as some individual of sardonic temper once remarked, "There are three forms of lies: lies, d——d lies, and statistics, and the worst of the three are statistics!"

V I

IRELAND

I. Kingstown to Rosslare

"Know'st thou the land where the mists are drawn,
O'er the face of eve and the face of dawn,
Where the wild hill sleeps as the wide mist creeps,
And weeping wakes and waking weeps;
Where the maids are picturesquely dressed,
And their cheeks are caressed by the wet south-west;
Where the pig in the bog for potatoes digs,
And the people partake of potatoes and pigs;
Where, twilight and noon, the old wives croon
Of the land that lies beyond all eyes,
East of the sun and west of the moon?
'I do be thinking,' the maiden said,
"Tis easy sailing from Holyhead."'   F. S.

IN the heart of an owner unable by reason of
his occupation to execute personally the
fitting out of his boat or to superintend the performance of the man to whom the work has been
entrusted, the recollection of different winter
quarters cannot fail to excite feelings either of
moderate satisfaction or of bitter resentment. But
though there are places where I would lay up a
boat again only under the stress of compelling
necessity, I am glad after a review of many years

to admit that the majority of yards have given little cause for grievous complaint. As a general rule, the yacht has been treated well and her owner with consideration. Kingstown forms one of the chief exceptions, for there the *Senorita* was got ready for my coming in a thoroughly unsatisfactory fashion, and little attention had been paid to her welfare during the many months of my enforced absence.

At the end of August 1906, the remorseless flight of time compelled us to curtail the cruise in hand, and to leave the *Senorita* at Kingstown in the hands of a small builder, the only man we were able to find capable of undertaking such a trust. The harbour appeared to offer no convenient quarters for a hibernating yacht, and an uneasy suspicion worried our minds that the man, trustworthy as he well might be, was inexperienced in the duty he had readily shouldered. But, a stranger in the land, and ignorant of any better course, I closed with his terms and left the boat in his charge. When the time of fitting out drew near, I bade him to do all that was essential, but to go to no unnecessary expense. Though I wished my pocket to be spared, I had, naturally, no desire that the ship should be spoiled for the sake of a pennyworth of tar, and previous experience led me to think that the instructions sent gave him a sufficient latitude. He took my words too literally. Beyond slapping on a coat of paint and stepping the mast, he did nothing whatever in the way of fitting out. *De mortuis nil nisi bonum.* He died a few year later. Possibly his sins of omission were due to a misunderstanding, and it must be stated to his credit that no effort was made to charge for unattempted work.

On 29th July, 1907, I started from Southampton on the *Lady Roberts* bound for Dublin. The Irish Steam Navigation Company no longer, I believe, exists, and its vessels in the days of which I write, were called pig-boats by the would-be facetious. They carried, besides passengers, any cargo that came their way, but I never travelled upon one loaded with a consignment of porkers. If a man was in no violent hurry, and not over sensitive about the social standing of his company, he might spend a very pleasant time on the trip between the Thames and the Liffey, and renew his acquaintance with the chief ports on the south coast.

Half-way between the Longships and the Tuskar an excited steward announced to the breakfasting passengers that the recently launched *Lusitania* was approaching on the first of her trial trips. The giant liner passed us in a trice, and disappeared astern in a dense cloud of smoke. No one dreamt that she was destined to be sent to the bottom a few years later by a foul blow from a German submarine.

Sunset was nigh when on Wednesday, 31st July

the *Lady Roberts* steamed up the malodorous Liffey. Any one who has inhaled a noisome whiff from its filthy waters will readily admit that in "Sniffey" a painfully appropriate nickname has been found. With that picturesque misuse of language for which the Irish are reputed to be famous, the inhabitants of the city have been known to declare that the smell of their river is one of the sights of Dublin. Disembarked with my luggage I chartered a side-car, and, in the hope of catching a train due to start in five minutes, begged the driver not to spare his steed. The man agreed with the utmost goodwill, but the refusal of a sorry nag, in spite of vociferous encouragement and the spur of an active whip, to quicken a limping trot, spoiled a fine effort to emulate the furious driving of Jehu, the son of Nimshi. "Pat," said an Englishman, to an Irish cab-driver who endeavoured in vain to extract from a weedy animal a show of speed. "I thought Irish horses were all blood stock." "An' so they be," was the prompt response, "all Irish hosses is blood hosses, an' this is the bloodiest of the lot!"

At 9.30 p.m. the train deposited me on the Kingstown platform. Guided by a boy shouldering my bag I was not long in reaching the dwelling of the yacht's guardian, and was promptly put by him into the hands of Tim O'Donnell, who had been retained to do my bidding, however late the hour of my arrival. Tim was a man of thirty-five to whom, as he rowed me aboard, I took with the utmost kindness. His rich brogue and quaint conceits were mightily amusing, and, though as yet I knew it not, he was fated to prove my salvation in the gloomy hours of the morrow. The yacht was found, and, with a promise to give me a look in the morning, Tim left me standing with my baggage on the deck in solitary state.

For a moment or two I lingered aft, and, with a proud sense of ownership, scanned the dim outline of the hull. But the night was cool, and sentiment is quickly routed by a chilly atmosphere. I lowered my bag through the hatchway, and followed it down the companion ladder. An exploring foot sought unsuccessfully for a clear space of floor to stand upon. By the flickering illumination of a lighted match a momentary view was snatched of the depths of the cabin. No man who is compelled to trust his boat for long periods to alien hands, ought to be surprised to discover on his first visit below, confusion in its wildest guise. But what the lighted match disclosed was not confusion. It was chaos chaos with a capital C, *rudis indigestaque moles*, as Ovid says. Sails, mattresses, blankets were all mixed up together. Books and cooking utensils nestled in close companionship. The barometer enjoyed the protection of a galvanized bucket against the chilly sides of which the binnacle snuggled with misplaced affection. The incongruous heap was weighted by a rusty kedge. All the yacht's belongings had been thrown below haphazard. Not even the locker cushions had been fitted in their places. When, by the expenditure of many matches, the state of the cabin was completely realized, I could only murmur bitterly, "Surely an enemy hath done this thing!"

The lamp hanging in its gimbals was innocent of oil. No paraffin can could be found by feeling in the foc's'le. At length, making as good an apology for bed as was possible in the dark, I threw myself down to sleep, miserably hungry and frenzied with wrath. My makeshift bed was very uncomfortable, and sleep refused to answer to my call. By 6 a.m. the work of clearing up below was in full swing. From occasional glances about the yacht's deck and rigging it was easily gathered that below and aloft much renewal and repair were both assuredly demanded. When the work below was finished, a closer examination outside betrayed that even more required attention than the eye had at first comprehended. My indignation was only slightly quieted by a good breakfast provided by the Royal Mail hotel. Tim was awaiting my return to the yacht.

"Is this the way the Irish fit out a yacht?" I asked in a tone of bitter contempt, pointing out the while the most glaring of the shortcomings.

"Fittin' out!" he replied with unconcealed asperity, "Is ut fittin' out ye'd be after talkin'

very rarely used in Ireland
→ *usually* *pronounce as Gael*

about? Be jabers, an Oirishman bates the world at fittin' out, or at sailin' a yacht eyther for the matther av' that!"

An explanation that no personal reflections were intended restored a peace which had come within a little of being broken. Tim explained that he had been employed only to assist at the launch of the *Senorita* and to tow her to some moorings in the harbour. He admitted that she was quite unfit to go to sea in her present condition. He pointed out further deficiencies that had been overlooked by my own eyes. The worst of these concerned the forestay. It was one of an old-fashioned type, fitted with a shoe, and showed unmistakable signs of breaking away from the shoe's encircling grip.

" Sure but 'tisn't safe," said Tim, "an' ut'll be playin' a dirty thrick on yez wan av' these days. But if yez gets me a faddom av' wire-rope, I will be fixin' ut up for yez to last out this summer. The job 'ont be nate to look at, but, faith, ut'll be sthrong."

He was engaged forthwith to lend a hand in putting shipshape the rigging of the yacht and he proved, fortunately, to be a workman of the requisite ability. Leaving him busy aboard I went ashore, settled the yacht's account, and spent a laborious morning in the purchase of sea-going stores. We concluded later that either Kingstown was an indifferent centre of supplies, or that the shops recommended by Tim were not the best of their kind. Though the work to be done was extensive, by sticking to it closely we had it finished by the late afternoon. The yacht was, at last, ready for sea with fresh lanyards to her shrouds, a patched up forestay, a new bobstay fall, and the replacement of the many odds and ends, trifling in themselves, but, in the aggregate, important to the working of the boat and the convenience of the crew.

At 6 p.m. the mail boat from Holyhead arrived, bringing Rouse and Duncan among her passengers. They were soon conveyed to the yacht, and, over tea, my tale of woe was unfolded to sympathetic ears. The story told and fully commented upon, our thoughts were turned to the more interesting subject of our future movements. The *Senorita* wanted a thorough overhaul, and it was easily decided that the cruise must end at Falmouth, where all necessary renovation of hull and gear could be effected. This decision settled the limits of our cruising. We proposed to work along the Irish coast as far as time conveniently allowed, run across to Scilly, and on to Falmouth at our leisure. The yacht had never before visited the S.E. and S. of Ireland, and we looked forward to the investigation of an unknown coast with all the eagerness of dauntless explorers. Unmindful of the disappointments of past cruises, heedless of the fickleness of winds, and forgetful of the frequency of bad weather, our minds refused to contemplate the possibility of adverse circumstances, but foresaw a month pleasantly spent on summer seas beneath caerulean skies :

"Hope springs eternal in the human breast;
Man never is, but always to be blest."

POPE.

The very next day our sanguine hopes were promptly damped, for the locker cushions sent ashore to be repaired were not ready till the evening, and it rained heavily and blew hard from S. till after dark. Tim, on his return in the forenoon from fishing in the bay, shot under our stern, and sang out that it was the divil of a day outside entoirely.

Saturday, 3rd August.—Our drooping spirits were revived by the discovery of a W.N.W. wind. At 10.30 a.m., under Tim's critical observation, with all lower canvas set, we slipped our moorings, cleared the harbour, and ran in bright sunshine towards the narrow channel that separates Dalkey Island from the shore of the mainland. Since then Dunlaoghaire (pronounced Dunleary) has been substituted by the Irish as the name of Kingstown. In 1922 a friend of mine, careless of prevailing conditions, took his boat into the harbour, and found himself every night uncomfortably under fire owing to the bombardment of the town by the Free State gunboat *Helga*. A soldier by profession and used to war's alarms, though the next yacht was hulled, he maintained his position from the 17th to 21st July, and then quietly withdrew to Wicklow.

Scarcely had we gained the open sea when the wind came up disappointingly from S.S.E., and set us beating over a strong foul tide. Soon clouds obscured the sun and the air turned chilly. Headed landwards, after a long board off, the yacht fetched a few miles to southward of Bray head. We had a good view of the town of Bray, a prettily situated watering-place of some pretensions. This is not, I am told, the place where lay the cure of souls of the vicar who so easily changed his religious views to suit changing times.

> "And this is the law that I'll maintain
> Until my dying day, sir;
> That whatsoever king shall reign,
> I'll be the Vicar of Bray, sir."

All the afternoon the yacht beat up slowly in a light wind towards Wicklow. Just at dusk the anchor was let go close under the land not far from the town. The harbour was reported to be easy to take, but, hoping to be off again early in the morning, we were not tempted to seek its shelter.

Sunday, 4th August.—Long before daylight the howling of the wind and the uneasiness of the yacht put an end to our slumber, and dragged me shivering to the deck. A strong S. wind, blowing parallel with the shore, had knocked up a heavy sea. Later it veered to S.S.W., and by 6 a.m. it had worked round to S.W., much to our comfort,

"Senorita's" hull, bow view

both mental and physical. The yacht was now directly under the lee of the land, and, the sea gradually subsiding, we were able to enjoy some sleep after an uncomfortable night. At daylight, lying in my cot in the fo'c'sle, I noticed that, whenever the yacht tautened the chain, a link or two was dragged out of sight through the chain hole. Its disappearance was unaccountable. At last my curiosity grew keen enough to draw me from the blankets to seek an explanation on deck. One glance solved the mystery. The cable had been passed only once round the barrel of the windlass, and one turn was insufficient to resist the combined pressure of wind and sea. All hands turned out in pyjamas to rectify this error, and the resulting chilliness magnified wonderfully the allurement of our cots. It was late in the day when we turned out for breakfast.

By 10 a.m. the wind was due W. and our shelter was complete. While we breakfasted with the content induced by a fortunate change in our lot, a big boat crowded with men came alongside to work the yacht into harbour or to rescue her crew. We refused shortly to be rescued, and jeered at their comments on the yacht's critical position. When they realized the impossibility of frightening us into accepting their services, they rowed away with broad grins, apparently amused at their fruitless expedition. The yacht was in no danger, and, now that we had a

10

sheltered berth, we were not inclined to exchange the privacy of open water for the publicity and dirt of Irish quays. It blew hard the greater part of the day, but the sun shone out warmly, and illuminated the pretty strip of coast enclosed between Wicklow and Bray heads. Some little way inland the Great Sugar Loaf Mountain raised high its pointed cone. All its sides slope away with a regularity which is strongly suggestive of mathematical precision.

In the evening, when the wind had died away to a gentle breeze, several small yachts worked up to the harbour from the direction of Kingstown, and we learnt from a passing boatman that the morrow was the day appointed for Wicklow's annual regatta. He attributed our presence to a desire to assist at so famous a festival, and was distinctly hurt to hear that the promised sport was insufficiently attractive to detain the yacht, if the weather turned out fine enough to permit her departure.

Monday, 5th August. — Our alarum clock had come to grief, but Rouse was awake at 5.30 a.m. and insisted upon our turning out forthwith. As we crept reluctantly from the warmth of our blankets, we bitterly attributed his early awaking to an uneasy conscience. The bar. had fallen a trifle, but the morning was fine with a gentle N.W. wind. Before, however, we had reached Wicklow head, the wind came up S.W. and set

us making short boards to round it on the last
of the N. running stream. When the tide turned,
the yacht was given a good cast off to sea. Wicklow
head showed up finely in the bright morning light,
topped by the towers of two disused lighthouses.
The modern building stands half-way up its
slope. The yacht made the land off a low rocky
point adorned with a rugged tower, which we
learnt from the chart was called Mizen head.
The S.W. corner of the island is formed by a
better-known projection of the same name. No
doubt there is a reasonable explanation, but, on
the face of it, seems as foolish for a country to
give the same name to two of its headlands as
for a mother to do so to two of her offspring.

By 10.30 a.m. the yacht had fetched in close
under Arklow Rock, and, though the day was
early, we considered the feasibility of sheltering
in Arklow harbour, for the sea was heavy and the
wind boisterous. Reference to the sailing directions decided us to let the place alone. A bar
that frequently silts up so as to be impassable
even for open boats offers little attraction to the
owner of a yacht of 6 feet draught. We braced
ourselves to face the difficulties of our further
progress.

From Dublin Bay to the Tuskar lighthouse
stretches an almost unbroken series of sands.
Between them and the land lies a passage available for small craft, but rendered difficult by

scattered sands and shoals of its own making. The big ship track outside the sands presented no difficulty, and we had made it several times before, but we were minded on this occasion to keep the land aboard and explore the inner channels. With a head wind, too, the possibility of anchoring for a tide was not to be overlooked. The Glasgorman banks commence near Arklow. Passing the buoy at its N. end we plunged along the channel that borders its E. side. The day was clear, and we had an unobstructed view of Tara Hill.

> "The harp that once through Tara's halls
>   The soul of music shed,
>   Now hangs as mute on Tara's walls
>   As if that soul had fled."
>
> MOORE.

At the risk of incurring the charge of unpardonable ignorance I am bound to confess that not one of us had the vaguest idea whether there was any connection between Tara's halls and Tara's hill.

Shortly after 2 p.m., reaching in towards the land, we weathered the S. buoy of the Glasgorman banks, and scanned the coast closely to pick up Roney point, under which the directions recommend anchorage in S.W. gales. There was no likelihood of a gale, but the S. running stream was done, the wind strong and the sea unpleasant, and we had been tossed about long enough to appreciate the temptation of a quiet anchorage. Roney point was, eventually, found upon our weather bow. The yacht was heading at the moment into the shallow recess of Courtown bay. Forward I was on the point of casting the lead when an excited yell from Rouse at the tiller reached my ears just in time to delay action. He had noticed that, close to the lead, the line was badly stranded. That defect temporarily repaired, I found 4 fathoms. On starboard tack, in smooth water, we crossed the bay, and, near the point, tacked into 3 fathoms and let the anchor go; while the wind remained in the S.W. quarter our berth was both comfortable and safe.

For unknown reasons the name of the point tickled our fancies. It reminded Rouse of Annie Laurie, and by an incomprehensible mental process brought to my memory the chorus of a song which I had often shouted in my far-off youth at smoking concerts and functions of like character:

> "Daisy, Daisy, give me your answer do!
> I'm half crazy all for the love of you.
> It won't be a stylish marriage,
> I can't afford a carriage,
> But you'll look sweet
> On the back seat
> Of a bicycle built for two."

Daisy's surname, I believe, was Rooney, but I may be quite mistaken. Duncan was very sarcastic. He accused Rouse of flabby sentimentalism, and questioned whether my mental gymnastics were not a sign of weakening intellect, and declared himself convinced that knowledge of music-hall songs, like exceptional skill at billiards, was an incontrovertible proof of a mis-spent youth.

In the evening we were roused from a state of semi-somnolence by the sound of splashing water. The yacht was found to be lying in the middle of a tidal disturbance. The actual tide seemed to be sluggish, but angry wavelets slapped the counter, and jerked water upon the deck. The yacht showed a truly Christian spirit, she offered first one quarter then the other to the slap of the tiny wavelets, but refused to be irritated into running ahead and fouling her anchor. By dark the turmoil was over.

The tides hereabout run backward and forward with considerable velocity, but rise only 3 feet at springs, 2 at neaps. Farther N. the water rises 14 or 15 feet, but the current either way is barely perceptible at the distance of a mile from the shore. The meeting of the tides—the one pouring through the N. channel, the other running up St. George's Channel—is the cause of this state of suspended animation.

Tuesday, 6th August.—The morning was bright with a W. by N. wind, but the bar., already low, had fallen still farther. At 7 a.m. we left the shelter of Roney point under whole lower

canvas, and headed the yacht S. by W. along the
land to Cahore point. The same bearing brought
her to the N. buoy on the Rusk Sands. In front
of us lay a puzzling network intersected by narrow
channels. The sky had clouded over and the
wind was piping up as the yacht entered the
passage between the Rusk Sands and the Money
Weights bank. She passed the middle buoy
moored on the E. side of the former, and was
soon approaching another which was supposed
to mark the S. limit of the sand. But it proved to
be the N. Blackwater. The yacht was hastily
tacked, and fell in with some lumpy water as she
passed over the edge of the Blackwater bank.
The S.W. Rusk buoy was found, and, being now
clear of the worst of the sands, we laid the yacht
to and put a single reef in the mainsail.

In weather that grew steadily worse we made
short boards along a low and unattractive shore.
We passed some Brixham trawlers. They carried
their topsails, while we wondered how much
longer the yacht could stagger along without
further reduction of canvas. About noon, after a
shower of rain, the wind flew to N.W. and sent
us racing along towards Rosslare, where we
hoped to find shelter from the inclement weather,
Wexford was even nearer, but the account of its
shifting bar given in the directions was in no
way encouraging, and suggested a place to be
tackled by strangers only with hesitation, and

under conditions of weather far better than the present.

A terrible squall from W. rendered the yacht for a moment unmanageable, but Rosslare was already in sight, and, by settling the throat a couple of feet, we managed to carry on without coming to grief. In a smother of foam the yacht dashed through the N. Shear and past the end of the breakwater into the harbour. The anchor was dropped at 1 p.m. between the shore and a line of mooring buoys. The harbour, such as it is, faces about N. and with the wind N.W. gave only a nominal shelter. But it was soon found that there was an absence of tide, and that the yacht, riding head to wind, was little troubled by the short seas that came tumbling in. A scheme for running a rope to one of the buoys was quickly abandoned as being unnecessary. Everything below was heart-breakingly wet. The mast wedges had been so carelessly inserted that water poured down between them in bucketfuls. We caulked the interstices to the best of our ability and nailed a strip of canvas over the wedges, but we failed to stop completely the inflow of water.

The day was ended with a luxurious tea. There was on board a large store of eggs, many cracked and all of doubtful age. To Rouse was entrusted the task of preparing a dish of scrambled eggs. The dish, in spite of foolish suggestion and ill-timed criticism, proved in the end a huge success.

Cooked in this fashion questionable eggs can be relished by the most fastidious palate.

Bad weather detained us at Rosslare for a couple of days. The place is a bit of the Back o' Beyond, desolate, wind-swept, and mournfully uninteresting. A row of bungalows suggested the possibility of visitors. If any were present they remained closely concealed. The day's sole excitement is provided by the arrival and departure of the Fishguard boats. Still, in spite of its dreariness, Rosslare offers a convenient halting-place to vessels bound from Kingstown to Scilly or the Channel.

The first morning of our detention the pram dinghy was launched to visit the shore. Hardly were we embarked when, with laughable unanimity, we scrambled back to the deck of the yacht. The boat was sinking bodily under our feet. We turned her bottom up, and laboriously caulked with cotton waste a serious crack that ran the whole length of one of her planks, an undeniable proof of violent ill-usage. The boat carried us to the shore in safety, but admitted water freely in spite of our caulking. A gentleman and his little son assisted us to carry her above high-water mark, a coastguard inspected us with ostentatious suspicion, the proprietor of the only shop received us with delighted surprise. Alas for his hopes! Our purchase was limited to a box of matches each. Quickly tired of Rosslare we took train to Wexford.

Our purchase of return tickets recalled the story of the wild Irishman who, having conceived a dislike for the booking-clerk of his station, vented his spleen by the purchase of a return ticket without the smallest intention of making the return journey.

The centre of a rich agricultural district, Wexford enjoys a large measure of prosperity and, for an Irish town, its streets are remarkably tidy and clean. Cromwell's troops stormed the place and put to the sword the majority of its inhabitants. Somewhere in the neighbourhood in 1798 the rebellious Irish were defeated at the battle of Vinegar Hill.

" Betwixt Vinegar Hill an' Ballinamuck,
  'Twas there we fell in wid' a piece o' bad luck,
  For the smoke was so thick an' the balls were so hot,
  I kept runnin' about for fear I'd get shot."
The Kerry Recruit.

To show, presumably, an unbroken spirit, the City Fathers have painted up in Irish the names of the streets. We had reason to doubt whether the barbarous-looking words conveyed any meaning to the native passers-by; they are quite meaningless to the ordinary stranger. We had a cheap and satisfying lunch at White's hotel, where numerous guests of the farmer class punished the viands with ferocious appetites.

Our second day at Rosslare was spent lazily on board. A visit to the shore was prevented by the violence of the wind and the wildness of the sea.

II. ROSSLARE—DUNMORE—DUNGARVAN— YOUGHAL

"Upon the gale she stooped her side,
   And bounded o'er the swelling tide,
      As she were dancing home;
The merry seamen laughed to see
Their gallant ship so lustily
      Furrow the green sea-foam."

SCOTT.

Friday, 9th August.—The bar., which had risen to 30, had gone back a trifle, but we agreed, without enthusiasm, that the weather looked finer. A moderate W. wind was blowing. Up early, we did not hurry away, for we thought that weather developments needed some study first. However, soon after 10 a.m., we hardened our wavering hearts, and decided to start. The work of setting the canvas was interrupted by the arrival alongside of a boat bearing a demand for 3s. 6d., harbour dues, from the Fishguard and Rosslare Railways and Harbour Company. The charge was paid, but with extreme reluctance: it seemed excessive for the small protection afforded by the Company's property.

At 10.40 a.m., the yacht rounded the breakwater, and, running with a fair tide through the S. Shear, soon passed Greenore point. There are plenty of dangers on either hand, but, thanks to an ample provision of buoys and beacons, no difficulty was encountered in traversing the passage. We next fell in with some very big seas near the Bailies, an extensive patch of rough ground, where the tide ripples fiercely, although the obstruction is covered by plenty of water. Near the Tuskar lighthouse we tacked inshore, and, helped by the tide sweeping round the corner, fetched Carnsore point, a rocky projection of no great height. The scenery about the S.E. corner of Ireland is pretty rather than impressive.

From Carnsore point westward to the Saltee Islands and the Coningbeg lighthouse there are numerous outlying reefs and rocks, not all dangerous in themselves to small vessels, but worthy of avoidance on account of the tide-rips and heavy seas which are met with in their neighbourhood. The yacht soon came down upon the Barrel's lightship. We kept our reach seaward for some distance. Eventually, putting about, we weathered the lightship, and held on for a while, in the direction of the Saltees. With a head wind we were not tempted to try the sound between the two islands. After several boards through lumpy water in a growing breeze the yacht reached the Coningbeg lightship, which, riding a weather-tide, rolled heavily enough to dizzy a spectator. The bar. had fallen, the sky looked unpleasant, a port seemed desirable. We had little difficulty in deciding to make for Dunmore.

At 4 p.m. the yacht was put upon the port tack,

and heading, N.W. by N., seemed likely to fetch
comfortably to windward of Hook point, 12 miles
off, the E. limit of Waterford harbour. She made
very good time to within 2 or 3 miles of the
point, the end of a long low promontory backed
in the distance by lofty hills. Then the E. running-
tide came up in force and we were swept faster
towards the point than we drew ahead to weather
it. The wind fortunately piped up to greater
strength and the yacht began slowly to claw her
way to windward, but, for a long time, it was
doubtful if she would weather the point without a
board off. But, at last, we were able to bear away
a little. Soon the yacht was dashing through the
Race off the point. She scampered rapidly across
the mouth of Waterford harbour, and, rounding a
pilot boat lying to moorings, was brought up at
7 p.m. in good shelter off the entrance to Dunmore
harbour.

At this anchorage we lay four days in idleness,
held up by wet weather and heavy S.W. winds.
Anxiety to push westward crushed the small
temptation to utilize the time of waiting in exploring the Suir and running up to Waterford. We
wished to be in a position to take immediate
advantage of the first slant that came. The yacht
whose adventure at Kingstown has been already
narrated, at Waterford was commandeered by a
body of Free Staters. The owner was, fortunately,
ashore at the time. His wife and a servant girl

were sufficiently well armed to drive off the invaders after a battle of words. We found Dunmore a pleasant little place where life passed placidly and excitements were unknown. The harbour, enclosed within solidly built breakwaters, is situated at the extreme W. of the river's mouth, and faces the North. The directions speak of it as the resort of fishing boats from all parts of Ireland, but, during our stay, it was empty of everything except some local craft and a few small yachts.

The officer in charge of the coastguard was overwhelmed with anxiety about the berth we had chosen. He begged us to come inside the harbour, declaring with emphasis that the yacht was lying in a dangerous place, and that, if the wind blew up from S.E., her loss was inevitable. His statement, quite likely, was perfectly true, but we resisted his pressure. A S.E. wind was too ardently desired to be likely to arrive. To the crew of a small yacht the confinement and publicity of a harbour is peculiarly obnoxious. Outside, a man may bathe at his whim; inside, decency demands a hurried plunge before the world is astir. Our washing-up was always done in the cockpit. Personally, I am a little shy of undertaking this necessary evil under the gaze of critical eyes. Nothing rouses quicker the casual onlooker to unseemly mirth and ribald remarks than the sight of a man of mature years at work on greasy plates or scouring a frying-pan. Then too often arises a wordy battle in the order set forth by Touchstone:[1] the Retort courteous—the Quip modest—the Reply churlish—the Reproof valiant —the Countercheck quarrelsome—the Lie with circumstance—the Lie direct.

Led by Rouse we invaded the country round in search of eggs, and picked them up in twos and threes at scattered farms. The yards and buildings were untidily kept, but there were no signs visible of the poverty usually ascribed to the Irish countryside. We made the acquaintance of an elderly man home from Australia after an absence from Ireland since early boyhood. He had evidently lost touch with his people, and often spoke with pardonable bitterness. "They do be telling us out in the colonies," he said on one occasion, "that the farmers are squeezed to death with heavy rents, the people in the last stage of poverty, the children dying off like flies for want of food. And what do I find? The farmers with scarcely any rent to pay at all, everybody with all they want to eat and drink, and everywhere crowds of sturdy youngsters to carry on the race. It's a pity more don't come, like me, to see for themselves instead of listening to the idle tales of self-interested politicians." Maybe, but most of us, like Nelson, have a convenient blind eye to cast upon what we have no desire to see.

[1] *As You Like it*, v. 4.

The Ireland of the present day is a vastly different place culturally and economically from that of even 40 years ago

Wednesday, 14*th August*.—It blew hard at times during the night, but Rouse, on turning out at 7 a.m., reported with jubilation a light W. wind. At 9 a.m. we started with considerable hesitation, for, though the wind was still only a gentle breeze, we saw nothing to encourage us to hope for better weather. The yacht ran immediately into thick haze and heavy rain. An Italian steam-boat went by with wailing siren. For some time the yacht was kept with her head seawards. The haze gradually lifted, and the rain ceased, but the weather remained heavy and dull.

At 11.30 a.m., on the port tack, we fetched Brownstown head the E. boundary of Tramore bay, a shallow inlet liable to be mistaken in thick weather for the entrance to Waterford harbour. To lessen the chance of error Brownstown head is marked by two lofty towers. Great Newton head, at the W. end of the bay, supports three towers, on one of which stands the gigantic figure of a man with left arm outstretched in the direction of Waterford. Before the erection of these marks, even when the weather was clear, many a vessel, imagining herself to be hastening into safety, rushed headlong to unanticipated destruction.

All the afternoon the yacht was worked slowly to windward. The tide hereabouts is too weak to require attention, but the wind, though it flawed about, remained persistently ahead. At 6 p.m.

we were lying becalmed close to Carricknamoan Island, a mass of rock lying off Ballinacourty point, the E. extremity of Dungarvan Bay, where in the unsettled state of the weather it seemed wise to seek shelter for the night. This harbour is a terrible fraud. The wide expanse of water visible at high tide contains but one spot, named the Pool, 2 miles below the town, where a vessel can lie afloat in shelter. At Dungarvan quays the river runs almost dry.

A heavy shower of rain brought a N.W. breeze of unnecessary strength. The yacht reached across the bay on starboard tack past the Carrickapane rock, which faces the centre of the entrance, and, when tacked, fetched, in a heavy squall, right up to Ballinacourty pier. The anchor was let go at 7.30 p.m. in insufficient water, for we had slightly overshot the anchoring ground. Directed by a couple of men, we shifted to a berth off the coast-guard station, only with difficulty were our visitors persuaded to relieve us of their presence. They seemed to regard the yacht as treasure trove. A generous allowance of whisky was bestowed, and, when at last they realized there was nothing to be wheedled out of us in the way of "an ould sail or a thrifle of rope or a lick of paint," they bade us an unwilling farewell, and rowed away into the growing darkness.

Thursday, 15*th August.*—When we made sail at 9 a.m., the wind, N.W., was so light that we were

11

sorely tempted to set the topsail. But, though it wanted an airing badly, we fortunately forebore. After running out between Carrickapane rock and Helvick head we skirted a coast of lofty cliffs. The water beneath them was smooth, but such heavy gusts descended from their summits that, for the sake of comfort, a reef was tied down in the mainsail. A fair wind carried us to Mine head, a precipitous headland on whose summit stands a lighthouse. Thereafter, with water still smooth and wind less gusty, the yacht close-hauled headed W. almost parallel with the land. Crossing Ardmore bay she passed Ram head, the E. boundary of Youghal bay at noon. Youghal was our immediate destination. Friends—an old boy and his parents—were staying there, and a promise had been made to visit them.

Youghal has two bars, both carrying but little water, and certainly impracticable on the ebb with a wind blowing strongly down the river. We calculated that not before 5 p.m. would there be sufficient water for us to attempt either without undue risk. For the whole afternoon, between Capel Island, the W. barrier of the bay, and the entrance to the harbour, the yacht was laid-to or dodged about. The wind piped up strongly and the second reef was pulled down. Shortly before 5 p.m., with our hearts in our mouths, we tackled the E. bar, and the yacht was worked up the river abreast of the town quicker than expectation promised, for, though the wind blew directly down the harbour, a rampageous tide swept us bodily to windward. The only yacht visible was sheering about madly. We went a little way above the town, dropped the mainsail, and, running back slowly under the jib, picked up with deliberation a berth off the lightboat house. The kedge was run away at once, and the yacht safely moored.

In the evening we landed to find my friends. Their address had been mislaid, but I knew within a little the situation of the house, and a kind-hearted grocer was able to give exact information. Unfortunately only the boy and his sister were at home. We had confidently expected an invitation to the evening meal, and, disappointed, returned to the yacht in chastened mood. The town was evidently a military centre. The streets were full of kilted warriors, objects of interest to shy colleens. We found the dinghy in the hands of a crowd of boys who wisely fled at our approach.

III. Youghal—Crosshaven—Kinsale— Scilly—Falmouth

Heavy rain ushered in the following morning, and a S.W. wind blustered furiously all day. My friends, *père et fils*, took advantage of a lull to pay the yacht a visit, and pressed the crew to join them at that night's dinner. But when we learnt that other guests had been invited, we pointed out that our best yachting clothes would bring shyness upon the wearers and discomfort upon our hosts. An invitation to breakfast the next morning was considerately substituted. Rouse and Duncan spent most of the time ashore in spite of pouring rain. Though its bathing attracts a number of visitors, Youghal is not a place of absorbing interest. Pleasantly situated on the side of a hill it is said to be a town of no mushroom growth, and boasts in its midst a house which was once the home of Sir Walter Raleigh. Can it have been an excited native of Youghal who, unless this is yet another legend fabricated for the deception of children, deluged his master with a bucketful of water the first time he was seen with a lighted cigar between his lips? And was it in a Youghal garden that the first crop of potatoes was raised in Ireland?

Saturday, 17*th August.*—Beautified to the utmost limit of our powers, we made our way at the appointed time to Clay Castle. Our host was laid up with a serious cold, but sympathy with our host was soon forgotten in the delights of a luxurious breakfast. His wife and children loaded our plates with toothsome foods. All valiant trenchermen, we began the feast without diffidence, but, before long, our hunger sated, we were constrained to cry with Macbeth, "Hold, enough!" In vain. No sooner was one dish cleared than another took its place, and we were called upon to make a fresh endeavour. Never before had we enjoyed such a meal. This was a red-letter day in the lives of three men. "Thank the Lord," whispered Duncan, "it is not our job to wash the plates and dishes up."

At last, replete and lethargic, we took leave of our friends, and with deliberate steps and hard puffing of pipes, began a dilatory progress back to the yacht. We paused awhile to gaze with amusement upon the antics of bathers gaily disporting upon the sandy shore. A trio attracted all our attention. Two ladies of portly build dragged an unwilling child between them into the water. Their bathing costumes appeared to the inexperienced eye to be simply white nightdresses pressed into service. The higher these were wetted, the closer they clung to the persons of the wearers, and the result was an unconventional display of the human form divine. The scene impressed upon us the wisdom of the priests who, at least in Ireland, refuse to countenance the habit of mixed bathing.

We changed into working-clothes, and were soon under way. The bottom of the harbour is said to be hard, but both our anchors had a stubborn hold. The wind, W. by S., was strong enough to justify the reef which was put in the mainsail. At 11.40 a.m. the yacht cleared the river, and, as the hour of high water was yet barely past, she was boldly sailed across the banks, and then kept on a reach seaward for several miles. H.M.S. *Skipjack*, a gunboat often seen in Harwich waters, passed across our bows, and the officer on the bridge, noting our R.H.Y.C. burgee, turned on his binoculars and waved a greeting. The wind fell lighter, and the reef was shaken out. After a board or two the wind considerately freed, allowing us to head straight for Ballycotton harbour, the next place on our list of ports to be visited.

Drawing near to the entrance we were much pestered by proffers of assistance from men knocking about in boats outside. We refused all help, and, sailing straight in, were soon brought up with the anchor ahead and a stern rope to a pier. The bay, protected at its W. end by Ballycotton Islands, was perfectly smooth, and we should have been just as comfortable outside, and have escaped, withal, the recurring nuisance of slacking our stern-fast to let craft pass. The harbour is but a small enclosure of shallow water. Ballycotton is one of the shrines to which sea-fishing enthusiasts repair in crowds. The other two foregathered with many of the fraternity in an hotel ashore, but returned to the yacht hopelessly tongue-tied, so far as fishing-stories were concerned. It was incredible that they had spent more than an hour in the society of men exchanging reminiscences—a class of men, too, who, even more than golfers, acknowledge the pull of imagination—without hearing a single story worthy of repetition. I was sadly disappointed. To brighten my moodiness, Rouse did, in the end, tell a fishing story. I have never heard it before, but I have no doubt that it is of hoary antiquity. All stories are!

"A man, furnished with a five-guinea rod and the very latest and most expensive novelties in the way of lines and flies, whipped a promising stream a whole day without the encouragement even of a single rise. When, in the evening, weary and disgusted, he was putting together the paraphernalia to return to his hotel, a small boy appeared to fish with nothing better in his hand than a hop-pole, a length of whipcord, a bent pin and a worm."

"I know," interrupted Duncan, "he promptly catches a fish—triumph of rustic simplicity over plutocratic arrogance!"

"Shut up! Don't be so hasty with your moral. As you suggest, he does get a bite, and hoicks a fine fish over his head into the middle of the meadow. He hurries home with his prize."

"Well, Johnny," says his mother, "you have not been long. What do you call that?"

"Well, Mother," the innocent child replied doubtfully, "I call it a trout, but the gentleman who saw me catch it said he was darned if it wasn't the 'd——d limit!'"

Sunday, 18th August.—We slipped away at 9.30 a.m. under all lower canvas, and, after rounding the islands, began to beat against a pleasant breeze from W. by S. over the sparkling waters that lay between us and Cork harbour. Fine weather continued till the yacht was half-way between Power head and Roche point, round the end of which lies the harbour's mouth. We looked like weathering the point when suddenly the wind drew ahead and blew hard. Two reefs were rapidly taken in. We had just coiled down and put the deck in order, when a cross sea flung itself on board, and wetted Duncan and myself from head to foot. We were exceedingly cross, and our irritation was increased by the delirious chuckling of Rouse, who, standing at the tiller, had escaped by inches the unexpected inundation.

Quite a brief inspection of the chart and cursory reading of the directions assured us that Cork harbour, desirable haven though it might be for ships of war and Atlantic liners, offered neither comfort nor safety to craft so small as the *Senorita*. But into it from the W. runs the little river Carrigaline. The directions pay it the scantiest attention, dismissing it with the remark that Crosshaven at its entrance is the resort of small coasting vessels, and that strangers, to ensure their safety, must keep in the tide-ripple. Here we determined to seek a berth. After weathering Roche point we edged over to the W. side of the harbour, and, rounding Fort Camden, discovered the buoy with cylindrical cage that marks the end of the spit bounding the N. side of the river's exit. The ebb-tide was an hour off low water, the wind was puffy and baffling, leading marks did not exist, the tide-ripple was indistinguishable, and we commenced a beat up to Crosshaven in no happy mood. But, with the help of the lead and the guidance of a passing passenger boat, the yacht was worked to the anchorage without touching the mud. The wide-extended flats through which the river runs do not seem to be exposed at low water. A crowd of small yachts was lying off Crosshaven, and we let the anchor go at 4 p.m., well pleased with the resting-place upon which we had lighted.

The next day train was taken to Cork. There we separated, Rouse went on to visit an uncle who was spending the month at Blarney. Cork was found to be a fine city of broad streets and lofty buildings, but we soon wearied of sight-seeing, and at the first possible moment sat down to lunch at a big restaurant, and lingered over our meal to the furthest limit of decency. At 3 p.m. we boarded a train for Monkstown and finished our journey on the Crosshaven steamboat. Rouse rejoined us in the evening. He denied stoutly that he had kissed the Blarney Stone, but we were slightly doubtful of his strict veracity. We fancied that fresh powers of cajolery were detectable in a tongue already remarkably persuasive.

Tuesday, 20*th August.*—At 7 a.m. the yacht ran

out of the river with a N.W. breeze and rising bar., bound for Kinsale, whence we purposed, so soon as a slant came, to turn our bows seaward and cross over to Scilly. We passed between Daunt's Rock and the land. Our eyes were delighted by the sight of two magnificent sailing ships rounding the lightship to make for Cork harbour. Our passage to Kinsale was as pleasant as uneventful. We found a beautiful harbour, approached from the point of view of a large vessel by a somewhat narrow channel, but it is well buoyed and presents little difficulty to smaller craft. The town, a poor place without striking features, skirts the shores of a lagoon which is almost dry at low water. It has fallen from high estate upon evil days, for, a century ago, it was the chief port in the S. of Ireland, Cork has stolen the trade and left to Kinsale only the memory of its former importance.

We anchored off the town at 11 a.m. and spent the afternoon in securing supplies and preparing for our passage.

Wednesday, 21st August.—When we turned out at 6 a.m. there was not a breath of wind, but, after setting the canvas, we allowed the yacht to drift out with the tide while a breakfast of fresh herring was cooked and eaten. Nearing the sea we met a well-manned open fishing boat making its way up under oars. "Fine morning!" one of us shouted. "Eh, a fine morning, glory be to

God!" replied the helmsman, who divided his attention between the tiller and a clumsy oar. But his pious words were no proof of deep-seated piety. Before we were out of hearing he was cursing his crew with quaintly-phrased but ear-startling blasphemy.

Once out of the harbour the yacht felt a slight wind from N.N.W. and as soon as we found it meant to stay, the topsail was set for the first time since our departure from Kingstown. At 9.15 a.m. the Old Head of Kinsale bore W., distant 3 miles, and the yacht was put upon the course S.S.E. for Round Island in the Scilly group. The wind gradually freshened into a fine breeze. From time to time it worked to W., but for the most part retained a touch of N. But for the absence of sun, the day would have been glorious. The sun managed to make a show only a few moments before the time for its setting. Except for a wisp of cloud before its face, it sank quite clear beneath the horizon. At 9 p.m. it was calculated that the yacht had run 60 miles. Duncan took first watch in a failing breeze N.N.W., directly aft.

Thursday, 22nd August.—Duncan's spell was up at midnight, but he did not summon his relief till half an hour later. In answer to my expression of surprise he explained that, owing to the loss of his watch, he had been obliged to make a guess at the time. He had by accident jerked it out of his pocket and broken the chain. He fancied he had heard it twice and finally light upon something soft. A thorough search showed that it was not in the cockpit. During the search a queer tinkling was heard in the port rigging. Rushing forward I was just in time to save the oil container from slipping out through the opened door of the sidelight. Investigation of the mystery of the lost watch was postponed till daylight, but Duncan was scarcely gone below before he was recalled for a moment to the tiller to allow me to look into some trouble with the jib. The pin of the jib-sheet shackle was found lying on the fore deck while the shackle still hung in the clew of the sail. As there was at the moment only a faint draught the sheets were reshackled with the utmost ease.

It was a beautiful morning—the moon, a day or two past the full, poured her silvery beams from a cloudless sky upon a gently heaving sea. The boom swung quietly over to starboard. Throughout my watch there was a faint breeze from N. Just before 3 a.m. the boom swung back again to port. While Rouse, ignorant of the night's occurrences, was dressing to take my place, he was astonished to find a watch lurking in the toes of one of his rubber boots. He scarcely believed my words of explanation, and, in truth, the flight of the watch from Duncan's pocket in the cockpit to Rouse's boot upon the cabin floor was hard to follow. It still ticked, and the glass was unbroken; indeed, to the best of my recollection, it was none the worse for its perilous adventure. At 7 a.m. a better breeze began to blow from N.N.W. At 9 a.m. our position was calculated to be 80 miles from the Old Head of Kinsale, 50 from Round Island.

But three-quarters of an hour later, the lighthouse on Round Island was sighted a point open on our weather bow, about 15 miles away. The yacht was, therefore, 30 miles, or more, ahead of our reckoning. The error was partly due to incorrect computation of her progress during the night, partly to insufficient allowance for S. set of tide. Our wind was hauled a point, and the pleasant breeze continuing, the yacht passed Shipman's head at 0.30 p.m., just over 27 hours for a distance of 131 miles, and was soon moored in New Grimsby Sound. The bar. at midnight 30.5 had fallen a tenth by daylight, and continued to fall steadily all through the day.

The next day brought with it miserable weather, and we were quite content to lie in comfort at our anchorage under Bryher. A fisherman, an acquaintance of long standing, paid the yacht a visit, and the purchase of lobsters was lengthily discussed. In bygone years lobsters in Scilly were sold on moderate terms, but, in these latter days, they have attained to a price which compels men of modest means to forgo the pleasure of crustacean banquets. An effort was made to cheapen the man's offer. The words of a blunt and tongue-tied individual like myself, naturally had no effect, and my appeal to auld lang syne was laughingly derided, but neither Duncan, a barrister by profession, nor Rouse, suspected of having lately had osculatory contact with the Blarney stone, were able to deduct a penny from the price demanded. Like the deaf adder that stoppeth her ears, he refused to hearken to the voice of his artful wheedlers, and, in the end, overpersuaded by our appetites, we consented to pay what we felt to be a shameful imposition. To work off a sense of defeat, as soon as the rain ceased, we landed on Trescow, and walked, so far as was possible, right round the island. Back once more at our starting-point, we admitted surprise at the number of miles that a small island can compress within its limits.

The lobsters were delivered ready cooked in the evening, four smallish ones for which we paid 3s. They were very good to eat, but no one, who has not made the experiment, can have the smallest conception of the difficulty of dividing four lobsters fairly among three men. Arrange and re-arrange them as we would, one portion was always larger than either of the other two. Their assignment was eventually decided by drawing lots. Rouse drew first choice, and, unhesitatingly, took the least desirable share.

Duncan, with second choice, left to me the largest portion. Though secretly not ill-pleased, I protested loudly against their foolish altruism. I have sometimes wondered since whether, if the lots had come out differently and first choice had fallen to my hands, I should have shown a like unselfishness. While I hope that my nobler instincts would have vanished greed, my mind is sadly harassed by the goads of uneasy doubt.

Saturday, 24th August.—At 5.30 a.m. we found the morning beautiful but breathless. We weighed our anchors, and, using the sweep to keep clear of the other craft anchored near, went drifting away over the flats with the intention of passing through Crow Sound to reach open sea. The tide had turned before he beacon was reached, but a faint breeze carried the yacht as far as the Hats buoy and comparatively deep water. From 9 a.m. to noon she lay helplessly becalmed near the buoy, surrounded by a bevy of French smacks. In the end a gentle W.N.W. air wafted her clear of the sound. The spinnaker was boomed out to port, but scarcely was it set and trimmed before the mainsail gybed and we were compelled to shift it to the other side. Then the wind came N.W., and with many groans we shifted it back to port again. It was too useful a sail to discard in a wind so light, but we wearied of the work it caused and eyed it with malevolence.

The wind sank almost to vanishing point, and

the heat of the sun was intense. Somebody was heard muttering the foolish lines:

"The sun's perpendicular height
　Illumined the depths of the sea,
And the fishes, beginning to sweat,
　Cried 'D—n it, how hot we shall be!'"

Our distance from the islands was increased only imperceptibly. They formed a pretty picture basking lazily, as it seemed, in the palpitating heat upon a couch of filmy haze. At 3 p.m. the gentle draught went so far N. that the spinnaker could no longer be carried. A light shower lessened the heat, but brought no improvement in the wind. A strong N. running stream swept the yacht close to the Seven Stones lightship. At 5 p.m., when the tide slacked, a better breeze sprang up from W.S.W. At 8 p.m. we passed the Wolf Rock lighthouse. During my spell at the tiller from 9 p.m. to midnight only light breezes blew, hovering between W. and N.W. A strong W. running-tide checked our progress, and vision was occasionally obscured by dense patches of fog. From time to time startling explosions reverberated from the lighthouse on the Longships.

Sunday, 25*th August*.—At 6 a.m. the yacht was lying helpless off the Lizard, the distracted plaything of a tumbling sea. The tide swept her in the right direction; of wind there was not a sign. After three hours of acute discomfort a gentle breeze from W. by S. quieted the racket, and

"Senorita's" hull, profile

held the yacht up against the now opposing tide. The breeze worked gradually to S.W. and acquired strength enough to force us ahead. Once through the area of troubled waters the yacht mended her pace. Between the Manacles and Falmouth harbour, we were compelled to pull the topsail down, for the wind flew to W.N.W. and blew with overbearing malignity. At 11.40 St. Anthony's lighthouse was abeam, and a board or two brought the yacht by 0.30 p.m. to our usual anchorage off Jackett's yard.

This was a cruise of the laziest type, and only two nights had been spent at sea. The unsettled weather impressed upon us the wisdom of caution, and the early fixing of the yacht's winter quarters prevented the onward thrust that usually characterized our annual outing. In spite of unsatisfactory weather and consequent delays we thoroughly enjoyed such exploration as we had been able to make of the Irish coastline.

VII

WEST AND EAST

KINSALE—BALTIMORE—SKULL—GLENGARIFF— SCILLY

"What land is there like Ireland
    To hold in sweetest thrall
The hearts of sons and daughters
    Let good or ill befall!
God save her, pray her children.
    Wherever they may roam,—
The green land of the shamrock,
    Wet with Atlantic foam."

JOHN STEVENSON.

AT the end of July, 1908, I travelled to Falmouth, where the *Senorita* was found lying spick and span, ready for sea, after the thorough and needful overhaul to which she had been subjected. By the time of the arrival of Rouse and Duncan on the afternoon of 1st August, water and provisions were aboard, everything packed away in its proper place below, lumber on deck neatly stowed and ready for immediate service. Our intention was to cross to Ireland, continue the investigation commenced last summer, and, thereafter, wing our way back, and up Channel to the Deben, whence we purposed to make a trip down N. the following year.

Sunday, 2nd August.—In the highest spirits we slipped our moorings at 9.30 a.m. The wind was E.S.E., but so light in weight that an hour was spent in reaching abreast of St. Anthony. The tide carried the yacht to sea, but swept her so far to leeward that a hitch off was necessary to weather the Manacles. The buoy was passed at 1.30 p.m., and, an hour and a half later, we had the Lizard abeam. The light fair wind cried out for the spinnaker, but the unstable equilibrium of our internal economy prompted us to eschew the smallest avoidable exertion. Even Duncan, the *robur et aes triplex* of whose breast usually enabled him to cry with the bold Captain Corcoran, "I'm never, never sick at sea," plaintively begged to be left in peace for awhile, "to give his stomach a chance." Our queasiness provoked many reciprocal taunts—but the spinnaker was left undisturbed in its bag. The cool of the evening was a delightful change from the heat of the afternoon. At dusk through the haze overhanging the land, Mt. St. Michael showed vaguely like a ghostly apparition. At 9 p.m. Rouse took charge of the deck.

Monday, 3rd August.—Rouse's relief was due at midnight, but till 1.15 a.m. I was left in undisturbed repose. Duncan's watch and his own were both in use as chronometers, and much too valuable to run the risks of trouser pockets. Mine, the hack watch, had for no known reason stopped for an hour. It was a beautiful morning with an E.N.E. wind. The yacht had left the Longships astern, and was headed N.W.$\frac{1}{4}$N. to cross the 167 miles of pathless waste that lay between it and Cape Clear island. When approaching dawn began to lighten our decks, my eye was caught by something unusual about the appearance of the bitts and the heel of the bowsprit. But no suspicion that all was not well forward troubled my contented spirits. I was not sufficiently interested to inspect the bitts at once, and by the time it was Duncan's turn to take the tiller I had forgotten that their appearance had attracted my attention.

The wind remained extremely light all the early morning hours. At 7 a.m. after a bathe the spinnaker was, at last, set. When that was done, I bethought me to examine the bitts, and stood aghast in the presence of what I saw. The irrepressible Duncan following the line of my pointing finger, murmured with ill-timed levity, "Bitts by name and bitts by nature!"

The bitts were all adrift, shattered, disintegrated. It was easy to see that the damage had been caused by a heavy craft swinging down upon the end of the bowsprit and driving it home. The mischief had remained invisible till the pressure put upon the bowsprit by the jib purchase forced farther apart the gaping fissures. Extensive repairs were necessary, and the question of the best place to seek for their execution was briefly discussed. The idea of returning to Falmouth was quickly dismissed. Kinsale was soon decided upon as a port within convenient reach, and a place fully capable of providing the yacht with new bitts. Headquarters of a fishing fleet, it must, surely, number among its inhabitants carpenters competent to do all the work required. The yacht's head was brought up a point to the N. on the course to her new destination. From the Longships to the Old Head of Kinsale the distance is 143 miles, and we hoped to cover the short stretch without the added affliction of dirty weather.

At 10 a.m. the wind drew ahead and compelled the removal of the spinnaker. For two hours we sweltered in a fierce heat. Thereafter a breeze of slightly more pronounced vigour blew from N.N.W. Bearing S.S.W., seven or eight miles away, the Seven Stones lightship was discovered, and, a little later, the Scilly Islands showed up dimly behind it. At 1 p.m. we became aware of a mighty warship approaching at a surprising pace. Passing close across our bows, she left the yacht a terrible wash to tackle. Her name was legible by the naked eye. She was the *Indomitable*, racing home from Canada with the then Prince of Wales, later King George V., on board. None of the royal party were descried on deck; at the moment they were probably at lunch below. At our own lunch we condescended to be sorry for the Prince; his trip was ending, ours only beginning. During the afternoon the wind was stronger, and for a couple of hours the yacht sailed her course N.N.W. at an exhilarating speed. At 6 p.m. our position was calculated to be 45 miles from the Longships. As the evening advanced the wind fell lighter, and during my watch from 9 p.m. to midnight calm was broken only by fitful puffs.

Tuesday, 4th August.—Throughout the hours of darkness we felt but little wind, and what we felt was not always favourable. At 6 a.m. the yacht was on the port tack heading N. by E. to N.N.E. Our dead reckoning made us at the moment 60 miles N.W. of the Longships. Yesterday till the late afternoon we had been parched up by a glaring sun. To-day the sky was overcast and gloomy, but the atmosphere was still hot and oppressive. A meridian altitude was gained from which the navigators, with a childlike faith in untrustworthy chronometers, deduced the yacht's position to be in Lat. 50° 38′ 0″ N. and Long. 7° 10′ 0″ W., from which point the Old Head of Kinsale, bearing N.N.W., was distant 79 miles. In the afternoon the wind grew stronger and the sea became troublesome, but the yacht on the port tack just headed N.N.W. At 5 p.m. her head fell off, and the increasing weight of wind com-

pelled us to pull down the topsail. By 8 p.m. it
blew so hard that the mainsail was double reefed
and the staysail stowed. No sooner were the reefs
in than the wind lulled and the yacht doddered
about rather lifelessly from 9 p.m. until midnight,
pointing N. to N.N.E. and making little headway.

Wednesday, 5th *August*.—Soon after midnight the
wind piped up again and the sea grew worse.
By 3 a.m. the wind was strong and the sea exceedingly heavy. At 6 a.m. it was obvious that the
bowsprit must be pulled in at once, for the crazy
bitts now made scarce a pretence of gripping its
heel and no method of reinforcing its weakness
lay within our power. There was no need to
remove the fid. At a touch the bitts collapsed like
a house of cards, and the bowsprit hauled inboard
with little exertion on our part. The staysail was
set, the yacht put upon the starboard tack, and
our hearts hardened to endure a few disagreeable
hours. The yacht headed N.W. by N., but soon
came up to N.N.W. The seas were big, but
regular, and, relieved of the bowsprit's projecting
weight, she made excellent weather, and topped
each surging hill without a sign of flurry or fuss.
Not one of the crew was physically happy; no
attempt was made to boil the kettle; the stoutest
stomached was content with a breakfast of a
morsel of biscuit. But unpleasant symptoms failed
to depress our spirits, for we knew that they would
quickly pass. What did inflict a morbid view of

life was the need to man the pump at the end of every hour.

To be or not to be, soliloquized Hamlet. To pump or not to pump was the recurring purport of our thoughts. Caught in this breeze before her topsides had taken up, the yacht admitted water freely. Of all laborious duties that fall to one's lot afloat, pumping in a sea-way is by far the worst, especially for men who are feeling none too well. To pump in harbour, when the boat is on an even keel, is wearisome enough, but to pump in an awkward attitude, when to stand solidly over one's work is impossible, is not only back-breaking but comes near to rend the heart. Still the work could not be neglected and the doing of it, repulsive though it was, helped largely in the cure of our temporary weakness. I discovered many years later that a semi-rotary pump removes all the difficulties of pumping in bad weather. Its earlier discovery would have saved me from many a miserable quarter of an hour.

By 10 a.m. appetite was beginning to re-assert its sway and we thoroughly enjoyed an early lunch of bread and cheese and beer. Bouts at the pump became less frequent. The sun burst through the clouds, and cheered us mightily. By noon we were quite ourselves again, and really found pleasure in the fierce wind and lively motion. In the afternoon the wind lulled considerably and worked round to nearly E. At 5 p.m.

the water was smooth enough to allow the kettle to be boiled. Our tea was a noble meal, although, not so many hours before, we had nibbled daintily at a biscuit and loathed the idea of solid food. In spite of the indisputable misery which the heave of the sea can cause, unhappy the wight, we thought :

"Who ne'er knew salt or heard the billows roar."
POPE.

Soon after tea I sighted the loom of land. The other two were unable to pick it up, and uttered jocular pleasantries on my powerful imagination, but, in those days, my sight was superb, and I was in no way convinced that my eyes were deceived. Shortly before 8 p.m. on the port bow land was unmistakably visible. Half an hour later, while the side-lights were being shipped, a double-flashing white light was picked up ahead. What could it be? We were confident that we had made the Old Head of Kinsale, but were unable to get over the fact that from it a fixed white light was exhibited. We hunted through the directions and Pearson's almanac for double-flashing lights, and found never a one. The chart was equally un-instructive. Ballycottin Island showed a single-flashing white light, but the light before us, there could be no mistake about it, gave regularly every 10 seconds a double flash. At 9 p.m. Rouse was left in charge with a N.N.E. wind to keep the yacht still on a N.N.W. bearing. We hoped that nearer acquaintance might solve the mystery of the phantom light.

At 11.30 p.m. he roused the watch below with the information that we were already right under the land and that, in spite of a double-flashing in place of a fixed light, he was fully persuaded that the yacht was off the Old Head of Kinsale. She was laid to, the cabin lamp lighted and a further examination undertaken of books and charts, without for a long time producing a thing to enlighten our bewilderment. At last, with a howl of delight, Rouse stumbled upon an over-looked note in Pearson's tables, which intimated that in the course of 1908 the character of the light on the Old Head of Kinsale was to be changed from fixed to double flashing. We were greatly relieved to have the mystery solved, but it was unfortunate that its solution was not made soon enough to allow us to weather the head, and reach the entrance of the harbour without beating.

Thursday, 6th August.—When I took charge soon after midnight the wind was too light for our short canvas, and, the tide pouring westward, the yacht just failed to weather the head. The wind fell lighter still, but I feared to set the whole mainsail, lest, with only a single headsail, the yacht might prove stubborn and hard-mouthed. On the port tack she did little more than hold her own. But by 3 a.m. the tide had turned, and

Duncan, who relieved me, was able, in spite of the lightness of the wind, to work well into the bay. Slowly we drew nearer to the entrance. Once inside the river a good tide helped us on more quickly. Approaching the anchorage we were delighted to notice at the W. end of the semi-circle of houses that compose the town, a shed bearing in large letters the inscription "Boatbuilder." The sight allayed the misgiving we had felt about the certainty of repair at Kinsale. At 8 a.m. we let the anchor go immediately opposite the shed.

After breakfast Rouse hurried ashore to interview the boatbuilder, and returned in a few minutes with Mr. Thuillier seated in the stern of the dinghy. It was soon discovered that we had fallen into good hands. Mr. Thuillier set about the work at once, and stuck closely to it all day. He derived his name and traced his descent from a French sailor, who, wrecked many years before on the coast, had married an Irish girl and settled down in Ireland. In spite of his foreign descent he was more enthusiastically Irish than many a full-blooded Irishman. His work was thorough if somewhat slow. He was assisted by an incompetent youth who would have roused anger in the breast of an angel. Mr. Thuillier, though patience personified, was irritated occasionally by his clumsiness into the use of mildly savage language, but he spoiled the full value of his abuse by immediately applying to the delinquent an affectionate "my dear." Abuse and endearment were both answered by a grin of portentous width, which rivalled that of the Cheshire Cat portrayed in the pages of *Alice in Wonderland*. The lanyards of our bowsprit shrouds were found to be stranded, and the jib outhaul washed into nothingness. Through Mr. Thuillier we secured fresh wire for the lanyards and the necessary rope. Lazily we employed a hand on a neighbouring yacht to do what splicing was required. He did it very neatly, but demanded a sovereign for a couple of hours' work. The charge was excessive, but was reluctantly paid.

Kinsale as a town has nothing of interest to show, but the harbour is pretty and perfectly safe. The scenery about the short length of river that leads up from the sea is quite picturesque. In the late troubles the Republicans held the town and signalized their occupation by burning the fort which gave an air of distinction to the East bank of the entrance and, if an eyesore to the Irish, a fine pile that delighted the gaze of a stranger.

Saturday, 8th August.—There was still a certain amount of work to be done, and our hopes of sailing away to-day gradually faded. But at 3 p.m. Mr. Thuillier appeared with his bill. His account, including the charges of tradesmen for wire rope, leathering traveller, jib outhaul, and bowsprit lanyards, amounted in all to only £2. The new bitts made of Irish oak, while not highly finished, were solid and strong. After settling our liabilities we had a little chat about Irish affairs. One of us was bold enough to stigmatize as brutally cruel the conduct of malcontents, who, to annoy an unpopular landlord, twisted the tails of his harmless cattle. But our friend refused to be drawn. He met the charge with a personal story. He told us how in his younger days he once travelled to London to see the sights, and was shown in the Tower the grave which yielded up the bodies of the two little sons of Edward IV., supposed to have been smothered in 1483 by the orders of their wicked uncle. "Now was that not a cruel thing to be doing?—to murder two little bhoys that had never done anny harm to annybody!" The moral he wished to be drawn from his story was, apparently, that, before the English imputed cruelty to the Irish, they ought first to see that their own hands were clean.

The wind W.S.W. blew with such vigour that we resigned ourselves to spending another night in Kinsale. But by 5 p.m. the wind had worked to N.W., a change which determined us to resume at once our interrupted voyage. Within an hour the yacht was running down the harbour with a gentle W.N.W. wind. A line of yachts and fishing boats came streaming into the river. When once they had passed we had the sea to ourselves. At

8 p.m. the Old Head of Kinsale was abeam. The weather was fine, the sea smooth, and throughout the night steady breezes never for a moment failed. At 11 p.m. a board was made into Court-macsherry bay. At midnight, on the starboard tack, the yacht was approaching Seven Heads.

Sunday, 9th August.—The early hours of the morning passed without incident. At 7 a.m. we made a board inshore, and tacked close under Galley head. At 11 a.m. the yacht was passing Glandore, a harbour which we had intended to enter, but the early hour and the beauty of the day easily persuaded us to forgo our intention. With a fine W. wind we proceeded to beat on to Baltimore. At 2 p.m. the yacht was some distance seaward of the Stag Rocks, a re-markable cluster which form an extension of Toehead. Baltimore lay a bare six miles farther along the coast, and we had good hopes of reach-ing it without another board when a provoking calm arrived, which brought to nought our san-guine hopes. But, at last, at 5 p.m., a fresh S.W. breeze arose which brought us quickly to the entrance of a harbour hidden by lofty cliffs on either hand. Passing through the passage left between, we found ourselves in a tranquil lake. Any idea of sailing up to Baltimore itself was in-stantly crushed by the sight of a quiet bight not far inside the lighthouse, which seemed to offer a perfect berth. Here in a few moments we let the anchor go close to the shore of Sherkin Island opposite to the ruins of an ancient abbey.

On coming on deck after our tea we were surprised to see on the shore of the island a crowd of boats, and their crews lounging about half-way up the hill, with their gaze fixed upon the restricted space of sea visible through the narrow gap between the entrance cliffs. We learnt that the men were lobster catchers and that a smack was due to relieve them of their catches and convey them to the English market. Lobsters were pressed upon us, but, as the men refused to cook, we refused to deal. Though troubled little by the finer feelings, and able without remorse to eat another's cooking, I shrank from the beastly task of torturing a living lobster by boiling it slowly to a horrible death—an idea, too, prevailed that the smell of a cooking lobster would taint the cabin, and offend for weeks our sensitive nostrils. Darkness was at hand when the smack arrived. For a short time bustle and confusion reigned. Then the boats rowed away to different hamlets, and the harbour was left to its wonted silence and solitude.

Monday, 10th August.—At 6 a.m. it was raining and blowing hard. The bar. had fallen to 30 from 30·4, where it had stood two days ago. At 10.30 a.m., miscalculating in our sheltered position the force of the N.N.W. wind, we started under all lower canvas with no particular destination in view. The moment the yacht was outside the harbour we found immediate reefing a necessity. In anticipation of a possible dusting we double-reefed the mainsail and substituted the spitfire for the working jib. The yacht ran quickly past the shores of Sherkin Island, across the mouth of Gascanane Sound, and along the precipitous cliffs of Cape Clear Island. This is a 3 miles long granite-faced desolate mass, from whose height shrieking squalls struck the yacht with venomous fury. We hauled our wind round the island, and anticipated beyond its shelter a troublesome sea. But the sea, though heavy, was far from spiteful, and the wind was naturally much less gusty than what we had felt beneath the land. Ahead lay the Fastnet Rock, bearing a lighthouse and signal station. Once the dread of the mariner approaching from the westward, this rock, now with its beacon light, first lighted in 1854, smiles a pleasant welcome and guides him safely on his onward way.

We let the yacht plunge on almost as far as the Fastnet. Then we put about to seek refuge in one of the many shelters which lurk in the recesses of Cape Clear Island bay. For a brief space the wind lulled, and we were tumbled about distressingly by the heavy sea. But the wind was not slow to pipe up again to great strength. At 1 p.m. we were approaching the E. end of Long Island. Skull immediately ahead offered excellent shelter, and was easy of access. In a smother of foam the yacht dashed into its still waters and was brought up a short distance N.E. of its pier.

Unknowingly we had arrived on the great day of Skull's regatta. The harbour, a circular pond, was crowded with smacks and boats, and the pier with shores adjoining was black with spectators. An anchored yacht or two dispensed hospitality to the *élite* of the vicinity. The crowd gave an air of excitement to what under ordinary circumstances must be a dull little place. The main bulk of the spectators in the evening departed by train—a train either drawn by a broken-winded engine which found great difficulty in making a start, or in charge of a considerate driver who brought his charge to a standstill when belated passengers were seen approaching in the distance. After several false starts the engine puffed out of sight on the road to Skibbereen. The bar. rose all the afternoon, and by night the breeze had blown itself fairly out. We hoped on the morrow to reach as far as Glengariff, which had been fixed upon as the limit of our Irish cruise.

Tuesday, 11th August.—At 5.30 a.m. we were fortunately roused by the noise of a crane working on a small steam-boat beside the pier. The morning was chilly but fine, with a light breeze blowing from W.N.W. By 6 a.m. the yacht was

13

under way. The breeze remained light and carried us only slowly across the bay past Crook-haven, Streek head, and Brow head whereon is erected a signal station to note the passing and receive the messages of Atlantic liners. At 9.30 a.m. we passed some distance S. of Mizen head, the S.W. corner of Ireland, swept upon our way by a racing tide. The actual head is low and un-impressive but is backed by Mizen Peak which, though a hill of only moderate height, satisfies the eye and counteracts, in a measure, the head's lack of distinction.

When the yacht was tacked, she headed N. by E. and, as the water was fairly smooth and the wind somewhat fresher, she appeared likely to sail direct to Bantry bay. Ahead gleamed the white beacon on Ardnakinna point, erected to mark the W. entrance to Berehaven, on our port bow we spied the Bull and the Cow, two massive rocks that stood high up off Dursey head, under our lee lay the rugged coast that stretches from Mizen head to Three Castles head. We crossed the mouth of the noble fiord known as Dunmanus bay and separated from Bantry bay by the breadth of a narrow peninsula. Sheep head, the termination of the peninsula, lay comfortably under our lee bow, and we had every hope of weathering it easily and running up the bay with a fair breeze in our sails, when, suddenly, the wind flew to N. and ruined our expectation. The nearer we drew to the point, the less grew the chance of compassing our object. But for once in a way we had a fine stroke of luck. When a moment only was left before the yacht must be tacked, the wind obligingly went back to W.N.W., and at 0.40 p.m. we succeeded in slipping round Sheep head with little room to spare but without the trouble of making a board.

So far the day had been cold, but now the sun shone forth and, as the yacht was running away from the wind, the chilliness of its touch proved less penetrating. Happily the weather remained quite clear, for Glengariff, like a modest maiden, hides its beauties coyly away and does not lightly surrender the secret of its harbour. But in fulness of time the entrance opened out on our port, and the yacht, at 4.30 p.m., was anchored at the inner end of a land-locked basin, liberally sprinkled with tree-clad islets.

Bantry bay is a sheet of almost tideless water which penetrates for 20 miles into the heart of a mountainous country. The day's sail had been very enjoyable, marred though it was by sundry minor disasters. Off Mizen head the parrel of the gaff-jaws burst and rained upon the deck its pattering beads which, before they could be reached, rebounded overboard and were at once lost to view. At lunch a bottle of beer was broken —a sad loss! And, worst mishap of all, the aneroid barometer fell from its hook, and, crashing upon

the cabin floor, died a sudden death from internal
injuries. It was a friend of long standing, and its
loss occasioned the deepest regret, but, when
some remark was made upon the difficulty of
repair or replacement on the outskirts of civiliza-
tion, Rouse cheerfully ejaculated, "Why bother
about it! Have we ever paid much attention to
its warnings on board this here old hooker?" We
had certainly never been slaves of the barometer,
and, while its rise was always hailed with satisfaction, its fall was seldom allowed to disorder
plans already arranged.

Glengariff is one of the beauty spots of Ireland,
and the man must indeed be hard to please who
is not content with the view that meets his eyes
as he rounds Garinish Island, or by the picturesque
scenery of the surrounding country as he explores
the neighbourhood. But the other two returned
from a ramble ashore more impressed by the
filthiness of the roads than by the beauty of the
scenery. "How is it that your roads are so dirty!"
a traveller is reported to have asked a friendly
loafer, as he waded through the morasses of a
western town. "Is ut the dhirt, yer honner?"
came the reply. "Och, sure thin, but Pat put in
for the job av scavengin' an' his cousin Tim on
the boord got him the conthract. So they shares
the money an' lets the scavengin' be. An' phwat
would be the sinse av botherin' about the dhirt
at all? If ut 's swep' up wan day, won't it be just

as bad again on the next?" Always against the government, an Irishman can appreciate as a joke the defrauding, even by another, of the ruling powers.

It was at Glengariff that an Irishman digging in his potato patch converted an ardent supporter of Home Rule into a bitter opponent of the measure. In the early 'eighties, just before the introduction of the first Home Rule Bill, which was destined to set Radical politicians by the ears and to bring into being the Liberal-Unionist party, he made a tour in Ireland to gather information by seeing for himself the state of affairs. A loyal follower of Gladstone and a keen politician, he had little doubt that what he saw would only strengthen, if that were possible, the conviction already firmly held, of the wisdom and justice of granting Home Rule to the inhabitants of a country ill-used and oppressed.

Even more unbounded than his keenness for politics was his enthusiasm for gardening. In the course of his wanderings he came to Glengariff, and the following morning, while strolling about in search of information, he found a man digging potatoes for his midday meal. The shocking state of the ground hurt poignantly the soul of the gardener, but he held his peace, and watched with wonder the methods of the digger. On lifting a root he put in his basket the larger tubers, the smaller ones he carefully buried again.

As the same procedure was adopted with every root, the astonished Englishman, at last, inquired with what object the smaller ones were buried. "Phwat for will I be buryin' the little wans, sorr? Shure for next saison's crop. Phwat for should I be pickin' um up an' be settin' um again in the spring when I can be doin' both jobs to wanst?"

For a while the Englishman stood petrified. What gardeners! Successive crops from the same ground! Not a scrap of manure! And the laziness of it all! On learning that the man was only doing what all his neighbours were accustomed to do, he returned to the hotel with steps contemplative and slow, but, hurrying home, he withdrew his name from all the political clubs and societies with which he had been associated, joined the Liberal-Unionists, and spent time and money in opposing the Home Rule Bill. Only to intimate friends did he ever disclose the secret of his political *volte-face*. "Home Rule forsooth! Slovenly gardening cannot but lead to slovenly self-government."

From Glengariff coaches carried excursionists to the Lakes of Killarney. At first the trip appeared attractive, but, when we learnt the time required and the expense involved, we easily persuaded each other that the beauties of Killarney were much overrated, and that the long drive was sure to bring weariness rather than pleasure.

Wednesday, 12th *August*.—Hour after hour slipped

by without the advent of an air brisk enough to
blurr the mirror-like surface of our anchorage,
but, soon after 1 p.m., with every stitch of
canvas set, we began to beat painfully out of
the harbour. Little flaws blew up from different
points, but always with a touch of S. in their
direction. Bound now for Scilly, we desired for
a day or so longer the continuance of N.W.
breezes. When at last the yacht escaped into
open water, the annoying calm returned and
held her fast for two weary hours. Eventually,
a breeze sprang up from W.N.W., to our great
content, though an immediate start for Scilly was
found to be impossible owing to the unexpected
discovery that the bread-locker was empty. At
the W. end of Berehaven we discovered Castletown
upon the chart, and hoped it was capable of sup-
plying enough bread for the wants of our passage.

At 5 p.m. the yacht was tacked, and passed
between Roancarrigmore lighthouse and the
reefs that encumber Lonehort point, the E.
extremity of Bere Island, and was soon working
to windward with a failing breeze among the
battleships that lay at scattered moorings in the
spacious harbour. One can imagine the British
tar, both officer and man, regarding with disfavour Berehaven as a naval station, but, perhaps,
both are kept too busily at work calibrating
guns and smashing targets to sigh for music-halls,
cinema shows, and the other amusements of a

lively town. At 8 p.m. the anchor was let go off the narrow passage that opened out into Castletown creek. While the other two hurried ashore to purchase bread before the shops were closed, I remained on board to stow away the canvas and to clear up the deck. They were back again before my task was finished with all the bread we could possibly want. They gave a harrowing description of the squalor and dirt of Castletown. It seemed to enjoy a certain importance through possessing the post and telegraph office by which communication was maintained between the fleet and the outer world.

Thursday, 13*th August*.—At 5 a.m. Rouse reported a flat calm. An hour later a gentle S.W. breeze was blowing and depressing heavily our spirits, but cheerfulness resumed its sway when at 7.30 a.m. a N.W. breeze began. Within half an hour the yacht, under all sail, was running through the W. entrance to Berehaven. This passage, owing to the high ground on either hand, is subject to baffling flaws, unless the wind is blowing straight in or straight out. This morning, with the wind well aft, we found no difficulty in running through. As soon as we had passed Ardnakinna beacon, the yacht was headed S.½W. to weather Mizen head, and, as there was some doubt of our carrying a fair tide so far, the spinnaker was set to starboard, although the wind was scarcely free enough to allow full advantage to be gained from the extra canvas. But at 9.45 a.m. Mizen head was passed with the tide still slack, and the yacht's head was forthwith put S.E.¾S. for Round Island, 161 miles ahead.

At 1.30 p.m. the Fastnet was abeam. The wind had grown into a strong breeze, and a biggish sea was running, but, though the wind was dead aft, the yacht, having the mainsail balanced by the spinnaker, slipped along with comfortable steadiness. The afternoon passed pleasantly. As Ireland faded from our view, we agreed that the investigation of its shores deserved more time than we had been able to afford, and we there and then determined, if we lived long enough, to sail back again and pry out the secrets of its western coast. At 5.30 a mist came down which saturated our canvas, but never seriously circumscribed the horizon. Before sunset the mist had disappeared, and the sun sank beneath the sea absolutely free from a veiling of cloud. At 9. p.m. the spinnaker was handed, and, as the wind showed signs of working farther N., the boom was gybed to starboard. Our distance was calculated to be 40 miles from the Fastnet. Duncan took first watch with a softening breeze, and Rouse spent much of the time that he ought to have devoted to sleep in futile struggles with his sextant to get the altitude of a particular star. It must be assumed, though the log is silent on the matter, that the moon was bright and the horizon clearly defined.

Friday, 14*th August*.—From midnight to 3 a.m. a stout wind blew from N.N.E., and the yacht, scampering along fast, spurned a rising sea with mocking heels. During the next three hours the wind was lighter, but continued to blow steadily. Thereafter it lulled rapidly, and by 8 a.m. it had fallen very light. The morning, dull and heavy, permitted the sun to show a watery face only at rare intervals. At 10 a.m. the distance from the Fastnet our dead reckoning put at 92 miles. The spinnaker was boomed out to port, but it did little good, for with a gentle draught blowing from N.N.E. it was difficult to keep drawing. About noon a better breeze sprang up from N.

At 0.30 p.m. an ex‑meridian observation, gained with difficulty and unreliable on account of a blurred sun and indefinite horizon, made our distance 43 miles from Round Island. With spinnaker now pulling hard, the yacht travelled fast till, at 4.30 p.m., a heavy shower of rain fell and killed the wind. At 5.30 p.m., having finished my tea, I relieved Duncan at the tiller. The rain had ceased and the clouds were rolling away. A few minutes later, glancing beneath the spinnaker, I was surprised to spy the islands right ahead, only 7 or 8 miles away. The announcement of my discovery roused only derision below.

"What land?" was asked.

Irritated by their disbelief, I replied: "Jerusalem and Madagascar and the north coast of Tartary."

But when Duncan thrust up a reluctant head to look, the gloom of incredulity which clouded his face was brightened by the gleam of satisfaction. "By Jove," he said, "Round Island and Men-a-vaur! I apologize, Skipper. We thought you were making a clumsy attempt to pull our legs."

But though the islands were so near, a weary time elapsed before we gained the harbour. The wind failed, and a spring tide swept the yacht relentlessly eastward. But at 7.30 p.m., impelled by a newly risen N.W. draught, we were drawing near to New Grimsby Sound. Under Shipman head we lost the breeze, but the tide bustled us up to Hangman Island. Fortunately no craft was lying in the sound, for the yacht was out of all control, and we were thankful to have in front an empty harbour. At 8.30 p.m., unable to manœuvre in under Bryher, we hastily lumped the anchor overboard in a berth too far up and in no way to our liking. Before the canvas was stowed, our fisherman friend came off. He thought the yacht was too near a rocky patch to port, and volunteered to carry the kedge away on our starboard bow to enable us to haul off from the danger. Swept away by the tide, he dropped the kedge upon our quarter, and it was therefore impossible to make much alteration in the yacht's position. What little we made, our friend thought enough, and we went below with untroubled minds.

VIII

THE SCILLY ISLANDS

"For as we stood there waiting on the strond,
  Behold! an huge great vessel to us came,
Daunching upon the water's back to lond,
  As if it scorned the daunger of the same:
Yet was it but a wooden frame and fraile,
  Glewed togither with some subtile matter:
Yet had it armes and wings, and head and taile,
  And life to move it selfe upon the water.
Straunge thing! how bold and swift the monster was,
  That neither car'd for wynd, nor haile, nor raine,
Nor swelling waves, but thorough them did passe
  So proudly that she made them roare again."
                                        EDMUND SPENSER.

THE Scilly Islands are the western limit of many a cruiser's voyaging, especially of those who through choice or necessity confine their cruising to the English Channel. And they form a fine goal to aim at. For, though they are not really difficult to reach, the passage to them from either Falmouth or Penzance is sufficiently long and exposed to allow of all sorts of changes and chances, and, at times, of sufficient excitement for the most intrepid cruiser. A description of a passage thither and some desultory observations on the islands may possibly be of interest as well to those who have already visited them as to those who have yet to make the venture.

The mate was prevented by the claims of his legal profession from joining the yacht till the middle of August. The *Senorita* had wintered at Falmouth. Aided by a neighbouring doctor, a man too well-to-do to trouble about a practice, I ran the yacht by easy stages to the Wight; inspected the French fleet, whose presence was the visible sign of the *entente cordiale*; and picked up the mate at Southampton as soon as he was free from the trammels of the shore. Then we returned to Falmouth. We had decided to visit the Scillies and thence to run E. to Felixstowe Ferry. For the following year we were planning a voyage to the North, and the Ferry would be a convenient point from which to start. The doctor, who had been impressed as a substitute, remained on board as a volunteer. He was quite a good fellow, but troubled with artistic tastes, a nervous temperament, singular inefficiency in matters nautical, and a terrific snore. In his sleep he produced a noise fit to rival the infuriated bellowing of a wounded bull. His wife, somewhat to my surprise, had urged him to undertake the absent mate's duties. Our first night on board betrayed the reason of her pressure. She was now enjoying a time of unwonted quiet; I was being driven frantic by nasal music.

Our first effort to reach the Scilly Islands failed.

We beat down to midway between the Lizard and the Wolf Rock, but were obliged at last to turn tail to a rising gale and run back to Falmouth. We were delayed there by bad weather for several days.

One—two—three—four ! The sound of the church clock reached my ears faintly through the partially opened fo'c'sle hatch. There was not the faintest suggestion of approaching daylight. Though we were lying close under the shelter of Falmouth town, frequent heavy gushes showed that there was plenty of wind in the open. The occupants of the cabin were both awake—I knew this well though not a word had been spoken. The mate had just emitted the combined sigh and groan which ever heralded his awaking. The doctor was lying absolutely quiet. Thereby he betrayed himself. Had he been asleep, the cabin would have reverberated with his snores. The mate began to move; I was very loath to leave my cot in the fo'c'sle. "Confound him!" I thought, "why can't he lie still till the alarm, set for 4.30 a.m., rouses us by its irritating rattle!"

Though a bulkhead intervenes, all his movements can be followed clearly. Now he is wriggling out of his sleeping-bag; now he is sitting on the edge of the cot gathering sufficient courage to plant his bare feet on the chilly linoleum of the cabin floor; now he is on his feet and with lighted match is examining the barometer: lastly, he

opens the hatch to its widest extent, and with
head and shoulders in the open air he is taking
stock of the weather. I await his report with
contrary desires. While I wish fervently to continue our trip, I wish with equal or greater
fervour to be left to the warmth and comfort of
my cot some while longer. What though I be
lying almost in contact with the chain cable,
side-lights, oil-cans, and the many odds and ends
that are stowed away forward, I would not at the
moment exchange my cot for the most luxurious
bed ashore. And 4 a.m. is such an unholy hour
for rising. The mate returns—now for his report.

"Skipper!"

"Hullo!"

"Four o'clock."

"Oh, by Jove, is it? Had a look out? (fraud
that I am!) What's the weather like?"

"Looks beastly! glass low and falling—lot of
wind W.S.W.—thick with rain. Don't think much
of it myself."

"What a nuisance! Let us wait an hour or two,
then for developments. Shove the alarm on to
seven!" And we all cursed the weather and
tumbled off to sleep again in supreme content.

In obedience to the alarm's call we turned out
at 7 a.m. and had breakfast, still doubtful about
the weather and undecided what to do. The
barometer continued to drop, but the wind backed
to S.S.E. The *Senorita* was a tough little ship; still

there seemed to be no sense in taking undue risks in a 6-ton boat. On the other hand, the fair wind from the Lizard onwards was a sore temptation. Human nature is weak. We succumbed so far to temptation that we determined to go outside and have a look at things.

At 10.30 a.m. we started with one reef down. In the company of several coasters bound to the westward, we worked out of the harbour. Ahead of us was a long string of vessels beating towards the Lizard against the adverse tide. The sight of them was inspiriting. Their skippers evidently did not anticipate any very heavy weather. Our wavering minds were inclining to cast craven prudence to the winds, when on weathering Pendennis and casting our eyes upward we saw an ill-omened sight—the S. cone hoisted as a warning to all whom it might concern.

"What ho!" said the mate. "What ho!" said we all. We were reduced again to a state of painful indecision and beat on half-heartedly. We passed the Manacles buoy. The weather grew no worse. The sky was dull and heavy and seemed to threaten rain rather than wind. We continued working to windward, gradually overhauling vessel after vessel. At 3 p.m., with tide now in our favour, we passed the Lizard and bore up W.N.W. for the Wolf Rock. The sea was lumpy and untrue. But the die was cast. Blow high, blow low, we were bound for Scilly. Any anxiety we may have

HENRY REYNOLDS

felt was for a time, at least, forgotten in the most magnificent spectacle it has ever been my lot to see.

From the westward there came close-hauled to weather the Stag Rocks a beautiful four-masted barque. Every sail that would draw was piled upon her. The seas that were tossing us about affected her not at all. She leaned gently over towards us under a very cloud of canvas. So close she passed that she took the wind out of our sails and shook up the yacht with her quarter wave. Fascinated we gazed till she disappeared round the Lizard. Save that she was built of iron she seemed to embody in every particular Spenser's beautiful description quoted at the head of this chapter.

The yacht went rolling on. Our anticipation of rain was verified. A driving mist turned into a steady downpour. We examined the barometer no more. On we were going whatever the mercury might be doing. We had overhauled all the vessels that preceded us out of Falmouth except one. Her we could not catch. She was a big heavily laden ketch. She seemed to be rolling her rails under. Progress about her decks must have been difficult. Possibly her crew wondered what life was like on board the little yacht half a mile astern. Our courses gradually diverged. She went off to round the Longships while we held on to weather the Wolf Rock.

14

At 7 p.m. we passed a mile S. of the Wolf Rock through a patch of very nasty sea. Just before dark we brought the yacht to the wind, took the second reef in the mainsail and changed the working jib for the storm jib. While, as far aft as I could get, I was struggling with the reef-earing, striving to keep a foothold on the slippery deck and hanging on by my eyelids generally, I was suddenly struck in the small of the back with what felt like an oar or a boat-hook. With tongue ready to hurl opprobrious words at the offender I looked angrily forward to see which of my companions was fool enough to be playing a practical joke at such a time. But both, tailing on to the reef-tackle, were obviously innocent. The blow must had been but the impact of a lump of water, but it was hard to believe that it had not been inflicted by something more solid. Under reduced canvas the yacht ran along more easily. The water was wonderfully phosphorescent. We appeared to be racing through a sea of fire. The yacht's hull was clearly defined all round by the incarnadined water, and her ruddy wake was visible streaming far astern.

We had rather an anxious time as we drew near to the islands, for in the thick of the rain we could see neither land nor light. We intended to go round their N. end into New Grimsby Sound. Exactly at 10 p.m. through the driving rain we caught right ahead the first glimpse of the red light on Round Island. We had made an excellent landfall ; all anxiety about our position was gone. Twenty minutes later we laid the yacht to on the starboard tack. We had been into New Grimsby more than once before, but we deemed it wise, under the existing conditions of rain, dark, and wind, not to attempt our haven before daylight. We changed into dry clothes, had some food, and dozed at intervals. The doctor went to bed in the lee cot. He complained of deadly cold feet. The mate discovered that he was still wearing a pair of heavy boots. He was hauled out and made to discard them and his wet socks. Then he went to sleep—to his great good fortune, for he plainly regarded the upshot of the next few hours with alarm. He slept through a very dirty night. He declared afterwards that he had not slept a wink. But we knew better. No sane person snores except when asleep, and he snored for hours without intermission.

Every hour we ran the yacht back to Round Island and laid her to again on starboard tack. At 3.30 a.m. we ran for Shipman's head, the W. boundary of the entrance to New Grimsby Sound, expecting that by the time we reached it daylight would be strong enough to allow us to see the way into our haven. But the wind played us a scurvy trick. It suddenly fell very light. The yacht was tossed about like a cork in the heavy sea. Under full sail and helped by the sweep she at 7 a.m. slipped in past Cromwell's Castle to port and Hangman Island to starboard, and was soon moored under Bryher's shore. We turned in and fell asleep at once.

After what appeared to be a few moments' sleep we were rudely disturbed by the arrival of a boat alongside. As, with a yawn, I thrust my head out of the hatchway, a man handed me a note addressed, "To the captain." The doctor was excited. He thought it was an invitation to lunch or dinner from the Governor. But it was only a request from some unknown lady on Trescow to be allowed to do the yacht's washing. We were cross—except the doctor, who had slept all night— at being unnecessarily roused from our first sleep, so we consigned the man to warm quarters and refused the petition of the lady.

The next few days were spent in knocking about among the islands. Sometimes we explored cautiously in the yacht, sometimes we chartered the fishing boat of the old man under whose house we were lying. Curiously, Scilly Island proper, whose name covers the whole group, is but a massy rock, scarcely to be distinguished from numerous other rocks in close proximity. At my first visit, many years ago, the islands seemed very disappointing. Planted in a rude circle round St. Mary's Roads, they have nothing to show in the way of magnificent scenery or striking qualities. They appear, indeed, to be entirely devoid of interest. But subsequent visits have changed my opinion. The islands, either basking in bright sunshine and summer seas, or rain-swept and pounded by thundering billows from the Atlantic, have a charm which cannot fail, slowly perhaps, but surely, to win its way into the heart of every visitor to their shores.

It was our fortune once to be lying in New Grimsby Sound, when there blew, for several days from N.W., a breeze that fell little short of a gale. To the W. of the Sound, and separated from it only by the narrow and fantastic length of Shipman's head, lies the deep *cul de sac* of water known as Hell bay. Battered and breathless we struggled on against the shrieking wind, till this maelstrom of tortured water lay at our feet. Big rollers, racing in from the open sea, met their forerunners recoiling from the stubborn immobility of the rock-bound shore, upon which they had hurled themselves. The seas, encountering like deadly foes, who in their rage had thrown aside all watch and ward and care for self-defence, met breast to breast and shot high into the air in columns and pyramids of solid water. Without rest or pause the deadly combat raged. The air was thick with spindrift and flying spume. No ship embayed in this death-trap would ever survive long enough to be broken to pieces on the rocks. The wind and the water alone would work their wicked will upon the stoutest fabric

put together by the hand of man—or so it looked
—and this was but a summer's blow.

On another occasion, one warm August afternoon, we were lying in St. Mary's Pool. We had
just read Besant's vivid and brilliant description
of the islands in his *Armorel of Lyonesse*. We were
tempted to visit Sampson, and, book in hand,
try to identify Armorel's dwelling. We had but a
Berthon dinghy, and the distance across St. Mary's
roads is considerable. But of wind there was
neither breath nor sign. We rowed across—three
of us in a 10-feet Berthon—and more, we returned
in safety. It was a rash adventure, which I should
not care to repeat. We explored the island. We
saw many black rabbits, and found several
ruined cottages. Not one seemed even remotely
to fit the description of Armorel's house. We
regretted our excursion. Cold fact took the
heart out of the novelist's romance.

Of course we visited the Governor's gardens on
Trescow. To the man who is learned in botany the
sight of Australian gum trees and of sub-tropical
shrubs flourishing in the open air is, no doubt,
interesting. To a man to whom, like Peter Bell,

> "A primrose by a river's brim
> A yellow primrose was to him
> And it was nothing more"
>   WORDSWORTH.

the sight brings little pleasure. I have always
found the collection of figure-heads set up in the

entrance lodge of much more interest than the
gardens themselves. In the grounds is a large
pond of fresh water. A pair of ostriches used to
roam about its neighbourhood. They are said
once to have chased a dinner-guest of the Governor
into its water and to have kept him there till
daylight. The story may be untrue. There are no
ostriches there now.

The owner of the boat we chartered was a
widely travelled and very interesting old man.
On the other hand, his son had never left the
islands. The Seven Stones were the farthest limit
of his voyaging. He was a friendly, but over-
familiar soul. A yacht with a paid crew he
understood, but a yacht manned by a sunburnt,
unshaven, ill-dressed trio of ruffians was beyond
his comprehension. Our faded and sea-stained
garments were a constant source of wonder to
him. "Merchant jacks," he called us, and confided
to the mate his idea that I was "a hard case."
Though, one would have thought, simplicity
personified, he had a keen eye to the main
chance, and between our early visits and our last
one the cost of lobsters rose from a shilling apiece
whatever the size to so much a pound and the
prices of fashionable watering-places in the
height of the season.

His father in his early life had been a deep-
water sailor, in his maturer years a Trinity House
pilot. On one of his voyages his ship rescued in

mid-Atlantic a crew of twenty hands. Short of provisions before, this addition to the ship's company reduced rescuers and rescued to a very small daily allowance of food. Still far from land, provisions failed them completely—starvation stared them in the face when, providentially, a passing vessel allowed them enough biscuits to keep body and soul together till they reached Falmouth, a gaunt and weakened crew. Piloting in his time had been lucrative. St. Mary's roads were crowded with vessels waiting for orders or waiting for a slant to take them westward. There were three or four pilot cutters and enough work for a dozen pilots. During the Franco-German war they received a heavy bounty for every German vessel they warned of the war and brought into safety before she was snapped up by a French cruiser. Now, save for an occasional yacht the roads lie empty, the cutters exist no longer, the pilots are reduced to two or three— and these do not grow fat upon their legitimate earnings.

He told us one thing about the islands which I have never seen mentioned anywhere, viz., that at low water of an ordinary spring-tide an almost complete circuit of them can be made on foot. A man can pass from St. Mary across Crow Sound to St. Martin; thence to Trescow; from there across New Grimsby Sound to Bryher and onwards to Sampson. A reference to the chart shows that this peregrination is feasible but scarcely possible within the limits of one low water.

On Bryher there are about 70 inhabitants and at least seven different forms of religion. Our friend, not satisfied with any of them, set up a one-man religion of his own. It was founded upon the literal interpretation of the Authorized Version of the Bible and was beautiful in its simplicity. Good works were of no account in his view. Belief alone was wanted. On my re-marking that devils believe and tremble he poured forth such a torrent of words and quoted such a number of texts in favour of his way of thinking that I retired from the combat at once, resisting, with difficulty certainly, but still re-sisting the temptation of making any allusion to Satan's proverbial skill in quoting Scripture. But he was a fine old man. He is dead now. I cannot but believe that in the Almighty's scheme of the hereafter he has found a suitable niche.

The people of Scilly, like the rest of the world, appear to be discontented with their lot. Yet under the fostering care and mild autocracy of the present Governor the production of early flowers and of early potatoes has assumed large proportions. And the sea teems with lobsters and cray-fish, for which the demand never fails. At the time of my last visit French smacks came over regularly to purchase all the cray-fish—the French, curiously, prefer cray-fish to lobsters—

that the islanders had for disposal. There are few
families that do not draw a livelihood from both
land and sea.

> "O fortunatos nimium, sua si bona norint
>   Agricolas."   VERGIL.

"O happy beyond human happiness had they but the
sense of their blessings, the husbandmen!

>   *Conington's translation.*

Happy surely ought the people to be on whom
both land and water bestow a harvest. But, no
doubt, they long for music halls, cinema shows,
tango teas, and other doubtful blessings of the
mainland.

We lingered on and we would have lingered
longer, but the holidays were slipping away and
we must to sea again. An evening came when,
with Teucer, we said:

> "Nunc vino pellite curas
>   Cras ingens iterabimus aequor."
>   HORACE.

(Now drive away your cares with wine; to-
morrow once more we will launch forth upon
the wide waters.) Margarine, we are informed, is
an excellent substitute for butter. I cannot,
personally, vouch for the truth of the statement—
at least, so far as I know: I always pay for butter
without, perhaps, always obtaining what is my
due. But I do know that whisky is an excellent
substitute for wine, especially when one's cares
are only such as prove an excuse for the glass.

With whisky we chased away our cares. Next morn we started and ran with strong fair wind to Falmouth, our first port of call in the long journey to the yacht's winter quarters.

The Scilly Islands are worth a visit. The man who has been there once will surely visit them again. The cruiser may approach them boldly, for the shores facing England are free from outlying dangers. For ordinary tourists, the unfortunates who are carted about by trains and steam-boats, the best time to visit them is, probably, spring, when the flowers are in full bloom and the new potatoes ready to be eaten. In spring, too, Annet Islands must be a sight to see, if permission to land can be obtained, for there the sea-birds breed in millions, and it is hard to move a foot without damaging a nest or crushing an egg. At all seasons strange denizens of the deep range about their shores, and the lucky angler can add to his trophies huge skate of incredible weight, giant conger-eels, monsters of 70 lb. and more, that bark and snap at their captors, and even specimens of the voracious shark. To obtain the last he must sally forth to a bank situated several miles farther out in the Atlantic. Siren Isles, whose summer is never oppressive and whose winter is only summer cooled. But for a moderate rainfall they might aptly be compared, in Tennyson's words,

> "To the island valley of Avilion,
> Where falls not hail or rain or any snow."

BEAU BRUMMELL AT SEA

"Costly thy habit as thy purse can buy;
But not expressed in fancy; rich not gaudy;
For the apparel oft proclaims the man."
SHAKESPEARE.

IN the days before road-hogs desecrated country roads and motor cars exacted their daily toll of lives, an evening in late July was sinking into a night more beautiful than what that uncertain month invariably provides for grumbling yachtsmen. Against the western glow were sharply defined the outlines of Orford Castle which, standing upon the summit of a slight eminence, seemed to hold in tight vassalage the little town that nestled at its base. The regatta over, the crowd had abandoned the quay and the vantage points upon the river banks to quench its thirst in the tap-rooms or to lavish its coppers upon the amusements of the fair. Orford's dull life was rarely stirred by hectic gaiety, and to the dwellers in the town and to the yokels of the countryside the regatta on the river and the entertainments on the land offered the only break in the irksome round of the revolving year. The usually empty street was thronged by a noisy eager crowd to drain the last drop of pleasure from its annual treat.

The yachts and smacks that had spent the afternoon in racing now crowded every berth along the uncovering mud on either side of the Alde, which, as though regretting its mistake in not ending its career at Slaughden, hurried along impetuously to throw itself at Shingle Street with reckless abandon into the arms of the waiting sea. Approaching darkness brought silence to the river. From the fair, the position of which was betrayed by the glare of kerosene lights, came, only slightly softened by distance, the sound of shouts and laughter, and a blaring organ; from the opposite shore, a part of the 10-miles-long waste of shingle and sparse vegetation that separates the lower reaches of the Alde from the waters of the North Sea, were heard but the fitful whisper of the dying wind, the rare pipe of a curlew or the whirr of ox-birds' wings. The quietude on one side of the river was in strange contrast with the tumult on the other.

In the cabin of a small cutter, anchored round the bend opposite the quay, two men, skipper and mate, were finishing their evening meal. The yacht was a capable boat even if she were not so nearly perfect as her fond owner imagined her to be, and she had never failed to bring her crew triumphantly through many a pickle with no greater damage than a lost bowsprit or a sprung mast. Like most yachts of the 'eighties, though she was not noticeably over-canvased, she carried spars unnecessarily long and heavy. The superiority of modern yachts is sometimes questioned, but never by the man who in a heavy sea has scrambled aloft to remove the topmast fid, or, soaked to the skin, has risked his life in changing jibs or bowsprit reefing. While the craft of to-day still have their imperfections, the pole mast and the stump bowsprit are in themselves sufficient to vindicate the evolution of the modern type.

They lighted their pipes and gazed malevolently at the crockery that must be washed up and restored in order to its resting-place. For a few moments they smoked, silently enjoying the comfort of repletion and a happy sense of freedom for a month or more from the tasks that kept them busy all their days ashore. With a sigh the skipper broke the silence.

"It is borne in on me that this is our last day of freedom aboard the boat. We know really nothing about this chap. As he is sharing expenses we shall be obliged to consult his wishes and to consider his feelings. It is more than likely he may prove a duffer and spoil the pleasure of the cruise. Misery acquaints a man with strange bedfellows, the poet says—and so can cruising, too."

"Don't be so disconsolate, skipper! It is quite true that we know little about the man. He was at school and Oxford with me. Though our families have been closely acquainted for years, I have never been very intimate with him, but I have always found him a decent fellow, troubled with a bit of side perhaps, but not enough to worry about. He has done a lot of sailing above bridges on the Thames, and I see no reason why he should not take to sea-work, as keenly as ourselves. Anyway when he volunteered to join the yacht I could not well refuse his offer unless you raised objection—which you didn't!"

"We ought to have waited for him at Lowestoft. Goodness knows how far Orford is from the nearest station. He will have the deuce of a journey to reach the yacht."

"Oh rubbish! He might quite well have journeyed with us down from Town. He is a barrister, it is true, and the courts do not rise for several days, but I don't believe he has ever yet held a brief, and the courts could have managed all right without his presence. Don't let remorse gnaw your vitals! We have had a nice sail round, and he will thoroughly enjoy an arrival in state. Unless I am mistaken he loves the limelight, and he will be the cynosure of all Orford's eyes as he passes through to reach the quay. Let us get these things away and have a look at the fun ashore."

Fairs as meetings for the transaction of business are no longer in existence, but in the 'eighties at any country gathering likely to be well attended

the steam roundabout and travelling showman
rarely failed to put in an appearance. This night
the centre of a waste piece of ground was occupied
by the former. Its engine, besides driving horses
for the bold and coaches for the timid, roused to
action the mechanism of an ear-splitting organ.
Since the early afternoon it had ground forth with
strident and maddening iteration the notes of
"Tommy Make room for your Uncle," a music-
hall ditty of inferior quality and undeniable
antiquity. Hard by were scattered booths for
boxing exhibitions, for the acting of tragedies,
for rifle shooting, for the display of obese women
and skeleton men. Outside the booths swings
were in constant motion. Aunt Sallies, and coco-
nut shies did a roaring trade, and the purveyors of
ginger-breads and ginger beer had never a
moment's rest. For a penny a man could test his
strength and for the same sum be filled with all the
electricity his system was able to endure. Cheap
Jacks rapidly disposed of their doubtful wares.
All was bustle and confusion and rude merriment,
for the rustic folk of those days in their lighter
moments were not mealy-mouthed nor was their
behaviour innocent of good-humoured roughness.

Satisfied with their observation of the surging
crowd, mate and skipper paid their pennies and
entered a booth to view the cleverness of a
learned pony and the mesmeric powers of a
white-bearded wizard. The mesmerism fell rather

flat, but the pony gave to the simple rustics vast amusement.

"Now you find a lady who is fond of a drop of gin," ordered the showman. The pony circled a time or two round the ring of spectators and at last nodded its head towards a clean old country woman standing in the front row beside the skipper.

"So I do, my dear! I likes a drop o' gin, that I sattinly do—in my tea!" cried the gratified old lady to the delight of the laughing company.

"You shocking old dear," said the skipper playfully, "you ought to know better at your age!"

After some further display of its perceptive powers the pony was bidden to find a gentleman who was fond of the ladies. The mate, fearing eventualities, quietly withdrew from the front rank, but the skipper, busily engaged in filling his pipe, scarcely noticed the order and maintained his ground. A roar of laughter roused him to the fact that the pony was nuzzling his waistcoat.

"You shockin' young man!" chuckled the old woman, whom the skipper had chaffed a few minutes earlier. "Who's a-larfin' now? Ain't you old enow to be ashamed o' runnin' arter the mawthers?" The skipper, without being a misogynist, was singularly unsusceptible of female charms, and disconcerted by unsought attention hurried the chuckling mate on board. Land often joins hands with sea in providing a cruise with embarrassing mischances.

15

The following morning was bright and the shimmering waters were scarcely ruffled by a N.W. wind. In honour of the expected stranger the yacht was cleaned up with unusual care and the little brass work she carried polished to the utmost radiance. Every preparation was made to slip away the moment the new messmate set foot on board. It was impossible even to surmise the time of his arrival. Wickham Market, the nearest station, was several miles away, and it was doubtful whether a conveyance could readily be found to bring him on to Orford. But groundless happily proved gloomy fears of delay. Midday was scarcely past when a nondescript vehicle, a cross between a gig and a butcher's cart, was observed depositing a passenger upon the quay. One glance through the binoculars caused the mate to exclaim :

"Come on, skipper; here he is!"

They manned the dinghy and pulled to the landing steps. While the mate jumped ashore with words of welcome the skipper remained in the boat holding fast to the quay and gazing up at the new arrival. He, erect with shoulders squared, looked down with an air of condescension and a critical eye upon his future skipper and the Berthon boat in which he sat. The dinghy had left its first youth far behind; the struts which kept it inflated did their office only reluctantly with the help of lashings; its canvas sides showed many a scratch, and the owner would never have dared to insist upon its water-tightness—but till the present moment he had not realized what a battered old tramp the dinghy must appear to a critic possessed in the slightest degree with a captious spirit.

While the mate busied himself in collecting the baggage the skipper regarded with a sinking heart the spick and span garb of the yacht's third hand. His yachting cap was of the newest pattern; his blue serge jacket, though it bore no brass buttons, forced by its cut and nautical hang the most indifferent beholder to wonder at the absence of these resplendent embellishments; his trousers with their suspicion of fulness about the ankles suggested in no uncertain manner the deep-water mariner; his rubber-soled canvas shoes gleamed with a brightness that would not have disgraced the snow-white decks of a crack 40-tonner; and his tie was what advertising haberdashers entitle the *dernier cri* in nautical adornment. "Jerusalem," thought the overwhelmed skipper, "he's rigged out for a voyage in a P. and O. liner—a regular incarnation of the late Beau Brummell!" Thereafter without his knowledge he was known by the initials of the egregious dandy.

Burly he was of body and brown of face. Command seemed to scintillate from his person like light from a first-class constellation.

> "The front of Jove himself,
> An eye like Mars to threaten and command."

It was a despondent skipper that paddled to the yacht an overloaded boat. "What are we to do with this fashion-plate?" he managed to mutter angrily to the grinning mate. He was not of a temperament to suffer fools gladly, while the mate, a man of happier disposition, was only amused by a display of garments suited to Southsea Pier rather than to the deck of a small yacht, and by a bumptiousness of bearing which a few days at sea would undoubtedly remove. It may be said at once that B. B. in spite of peculiar idiosyncracies proved in the end to be an excellent fellow, and was but a striking instance of the type of man who thinks to blossom forth a full-blown cruiser without serving a preliminary apprenticeship in the difficulties of seafaring, who dresses the part to perfection but is, unfortunately, unable to live up to the character implied by his dress.

His remarks during the short journey to the yacht were pleasant and sensible. He expressed approval of her appearance, admitted that she was smaller than he had anticipated—but what of that? "The smaller the boat, the greater the fun!"—and, his weight considered, nipped on board with surprising agility.

Only by the exercise of patience and manœuvring was his bulky kit-bag squeezed through the companion hatchway into the cabin. He followed the bag down the steps so precipitately that he dashed his head against a beam with sufficient violence to make the crockery rattle in the pantry. A badly crushed cap saved his head from deadly harm, but his scathing invective upon the ill-arrangement of a boat's fittings, which allowed a beam to obstruct the passage of an unsuspecting stranger, compelled the unhappy owner to see that a beam, far from being a necessity, was at the least only a booby trap and to apologize for its existence with disarming humility. B. B. soon forgot his rattled head in the pleasure of slipping about his limbs a pair of snow-white trousers. Incidentally he littered the cabin floor and both lockers with articles of clothing which skipper and mate submissively gathered together and restored to his bag.

The yacht was soon under way with all sail set. The N.W. wind was strong enough to drive her only slowly over the flood-tide. The Alde, in spite of its rapid current, gives good sailing water, though both shores are low, and the scenery, for the most part, uninteresting. The flatness of its surroundings ensures steady breezes. The tide was already ebb when the yacht approached the bar, usually difficult and occasionally dangerous, but traversing a temporary high water passage along the beach she was quickly shot out into open water. In the river the flood-tide had impeded progress; at sea the strong ebb had now to be stemmed.

"Can you box the compass?" the mate asked

B. B., who was contemplating with open vexation a smear of mud that tarnished the whiteness of his glistening trousers. Assistance in stowing the anchor had been cruelly rewarded. The mud of an east coast river is adhesive and warranted to spoil the beauty of light-coloured clothing.

"Box the compass?" he replied in a bewildered tone, "I boxed a bit at Winchester, but you cannot surely refer to the use of fists."

"No—can you give in order the points of the compass? N., N. by E., N.N.E., and so on."

Ignorant of this accomplishment B. B. set to work at once to improve his knowledge. The yacht, like all the long-keeled boats of her day, was easier to steer upon a reach than a boat of the modern type with its cutaway fore foot and consequent rapid movement to or off the wind. Bidden to keep the yacht on a S.W. bearing he sheered about wildly on either side of the given point. When the Cork lightship was suggested as a mark to steer upon, he succeeded, though with excessive use of the tiller, in keeping a straighter course, but he never acquired the art of keeping a compass course without the sight of an object ahead to assist his steering. Many a man, otherwise a useful hand, is afflicted by the same curious disability.

In the early evening the yacht was nearing Harwich. After rounding the bell buoy she had a hard tussle with the still ebbing tide to fight her way into the recesses of Felixstowe dock. The open expanse of Harwich harbour is an exposed and inconvenient anchorage for small craft, and the dock, only lately opened, was destined to save many owners from hours of grinding anxiety. In later days, when it was made a base for destroyers, it ceased to be a comfortable harbourage for yachts, but at the date of this narrative, save for an occasional coal-laden coaster, few vessels used the shelter of its piers.

To the uninitiated the first night spent on a small yacht is invariably a time of woeful uneasiness. B. B. carefully arranged the blankets on his cot, regulated the height of his pillow by a foundation of spare clothing and proceeded with premature content to put himself to bed. When with many sighs and groans, bumping of head and banging of elbow, he lay at last extended at full length, the pillow was under the small of his back and the blankets a tangled mystery beneath his feet. Frantic efforts to cover his extremities served only to increase the general complication. The mate came to the rescue, straightened out the blankets and, like a capable nurse, tucked him securely in. The light was extinguished and for a brief space deep silence reigned.

Soon repose was shattered by B. B.'s discontented lips. Every hour was punctuated by a fresh complaint. First, breathing was impossible through lack of air; next, he was feverish from heat;

lastly, the cold was unspeakable. His blankets had fallen to the floor and his unprotected body was chilled by the cool air that poured through the open hatchway. "When you complained of the heat I told you you'd be cool enough before daylight," muttered the mate unsympathetically as he snuggled more deeply beneath the covering of his own bed. In the morning B. B. wearily maintained that he had not slept a wink, but he fell upon his breakfast with a healthy appetite and soon forgot the misery of a restless night. The knack of packing oneself comfortably in a cot demands practice, and the restricted width is embarrassing to all whose experience has been limited to the spaciousness of a bed.

The morning, bright and warm, was almost windless, and only by hard work with the sweeps was the yacht worked slowly between the piers into the harbour. The last of the ebb tide carried her to sea, where the young flood and a faint breath from N.W. swept her quietly towards the Naze. The Stone Bench buoy was sighted, and with that as a mark to be steered for B. B. was entrusted with command, and the other two went below to trim the lights and to perform the manifold tasks that each day provides for the crew of a sea-going yacht. The breeze improved and the swish of passing water gratified their ears. Through the companion hatchway B. B.'s head was visible to the occupants of the cabin. His fixed gaze ahead argued careful attention to his duty. Suddenly the slatting of heavy canvas close alongside and hoarse shouting from unknown lips startled the workers below into dropping their employment and hurrying to the deck.

A big smack in stays was shooting past the yacht only a few feet distance from her broadside. B. B., with his eyes glued to the buoy, had failed to notice her approach close-hauled to leeward, and, though with the wind free it was his duty to keep clear, had made no effort to allow the stranger unhampered passage across his bows. Or, perhaps, like kings of old, he disdained the observance of laws passed to regulate the conduct of ignobler folk and thought that smacks and other humble users of the sea must without question yield the right of way. A battered old man at the smack's tiller relieved his overwrought feelings with cutting and profane remarks. His rude eloquence and power of vituperation proved clearly that he had mistaken his vocation for, good fisherman as he probably was, he would have made a greater mark in the eyes of the world and gained an easier livelihood as an exponent of communism or a socialistic agitator. The yacht was too plainly in the wrong to allow the crew to attempt rejoinder. They could only listen without a word and were unfeignedly relieved when increasing distance rendered inaudible the strictures of their contemptuous reviler. The last words that reached their ears were: "Go 'ome to yar mother an' git 'er to tie ye fast to a cheer! Gawd's trooth, ye ain't fit to be let out alone wi'out a nuss to look arter ye!"

B. B. was firmly deprived of the tiller, and after brief instruction in the rule of the road at sea was wheedled into the task of cooking potatoes for the midday meal. He professed to be an artist in culinary matters. Possibly he was not unskilled in the finer branches, but, like many a cook whose soups and soufflés are gastronomic triumphs, he was a signal failure in the boiling of the humble potato. Never again was he allowed to play tricks with his comrades' digestions. Nor was he ever eager after his first attempt to undertake the office of cook. The primus had not yet arrived to ease the burdens of unpractised cooks, and the stove in use offended his nostrils with its fumes and with its dirt sullied the cleanliness of hands and clothing even more calamitously than river mud.

Owing to the continuance of light wind the yacht dragged only slowly past the low sand cliffs that line the coast from Walton to the Colne. The flood-tide was growing slack by the time Clacton was abeam. They succeeded in pushing through the Spitway, but ebb-tide and dead calm compelled anchorage on the edge of the Buxey Sand not far from the Whitaker Spit buoy. As darkness fell B. B.'s eye assumed a wild and anxious look, and when a light haze blotted out the lights of Clacton, he clould not refrain from giving voice to his anxiety. He was unacquainted with night work, he admitted, but for all that he questioned strongly the safety of their present berth. Patiently it was pointed out that the yacht was far removed from the range of traffic in the Swin, that the riding-light was burning brightly, that further progress was temporarily prevented by the co-operation of foul tide and calm, that if the anchor were weighed the yacht must be swept across the Gunfleet Sand. He refused to be comforted and only with difficulty was persuaded to go below. He begged for a light all night that he might by reading help along the anxious hours. The skipper was already asleep in the foc's'le. When the heartless mate, wearied by his importunity, abruptly blew out the cabin lamp, B. B. threw himself down fully dressed upon a locker with the peevishness of a disappointed child. 'Twas no time for pyjamas and blankets this night with the yacht lying, a mere dot on a waste of waters, far removed from the comforting proximity of a visible shore.

In the early morning the wind piped up from S.W. and meeting the flood-tide raised a sea that set the yacht a-rolling heavily. Neither skipper nor mate was completely happy but B. B. was till, very ill. Between his paroxysms he asseverated almost with tears, that he had never been sea-sick in his life before, and that he was firmly convinced he was not suffering from sea-sickness now. The point was not contested. Whatever the malady, the patient was the victim of no light attack. Partly on account of the unpromising weather, partly through pity for B. B.'s distress, it was decided without any argument to turn tail in search of shelter. At 4 a.m. the anchor was weighed and the yacht with a reef in the mainsail was run back through the Spitway and headed up for the river Blackwater. Through the murk of heavy rain the Knoll buoy was discovered and soon the outside hollow sea was exchanged for the smoother water of the river. Past Colne Bar buoy the yacht sped with rail awash, her canvas straining, a hum in her rigging, past the Bench Head buoy, between the oyster watch boat and the Nass beacon, into the restful quietude of Mersea Quarters.

Breakfast was soon on the table. Crisp curly rashers, a triumph of frying on the part of the mate, fit to tempt a fastidious appetite, supported by eggs and cheering tea, failed to rouse the interest of B. B. or tempt him from his cot. Biliousness, he maintained, was the cause of his woe, and the best cure for biliousness was a strict abstention from food. Life on board, he was convinced, did not agree with his constitution. Strong as he looked, he was really delicate, and any irregularity in the time of meals upset the action of his gastric juices and was likely to induce an illness which might keep him in bed for several weeks. He expressed a firm determination to leave the yacht the moment he could be landed, and did not care a rap that Colchester was 12 miles away. If he could hire no vehicle to carry him he would walk the distance rather than spend another night on board. A very querulous and disgruntled B. B. he was—low in his soul like a child that is weaned from his mother, but quick to resent either banter or sympathy.

About 11 a.m. the rain ceased to fall, and bored almost to tears by B. B.'s plaintiveness the other two escaped to the deck to inflate the dinghy. While the work was in progress, B. B. donned his shore-going clothes and by this action in some measure recovered his despondent spirits. When they landed at West Mersea the smartness of his dress drew respectful greeting from a knot of longshore loafers. The greeting, graciously acknowledged, seemed to cheer him up immensely. Liquid refreshment absorbed at the Victory Inn, though small in quantity and non-alcoholic in character, restored him completely to his normal self. No more he spake of abandoning the yacht, but resumed the bearing of the bad, bold, piratical sailor who knows neither nerves nor fears—nor nausea. Biliousness? Why, yes— the hardiest are liable to attacks of biliousness— but sea-sickness? No, never!

Two days of indifferent weather detained the

yacht at West Mersea. When fine weather returned, she ran with a W. wind out of the river, up the Ray Sand channel, through the Whitaker channel into the busy Swin. By the time the Middle lightship was reached, B. B. was in a state of the deepest despondency, for he felt the premonitory symptoms of approaching biliousness, and had scarcely enough vigour left to take umbrage at an indiscreet remark from the skipper that, if life on board were not to his liking, he might leave her and walk, for, though the water was deep, there was land at the bottom. After rounding the Mouse lightship they ran down the Alexandra channel, and late in the afternoon were abreast of the N. Foreland. The yacht, with little wind in her sails and a foul tide to face, was headed to pass inside the Goodwin Sands through the Gull Stream.

A slight tidal roll increased the gloom of B. B. and impelled him to beg to be landed at Ramsgate. The skipper had grown so weary of his plaints that he was not unwilling to accede to his request. But the mate objected that, with their families intimately acquainted, B. B.'s appearance at home before the cruise had been scarce begun must cause surprise and might lead to unpleasantness.

"Confound the beggar," he muttered bitterly, "why don't he take his gruel like a man, not like a whimpering infant? He has not the pluck of a tame rabbit. A few days at sea will put him as right as rain and he will be grateful for the cruelty which kept him on board an unwilling passenger. Ramsgate be hanged!"

It was explained to B. B. that calm and tide rendered compliance with his request impossible. Dover then! At Dover he must be landed! To quiet his jangled nerves a call at Dover was agreed upon. With solid ground beneath his feet, B. B. was a sane young Englishman, but afloat he lost all nervous control and behaved like an hysterical maniac. Weak nerves were the allies of nausea. Sea-sickness, laugh at it as the immune may, is a distressing malady that can only be vanquished by pluck and endurance.

After collecting his belongings and packing his bag, B. B. turned in and fell asleep. At midnight tide alone carried the yacht past Dover. To land a passenger was impossible without the help of a shore-boat, and at that hour no boats were likely to be afloat. When B. B. awoke at 5 a.m. the yacht was a little way W. of Folkestone. Much to the skipper's relief he accepted without comment the explanation that complete absence of wind had brought to nought all efforts to fetch an anchorage off Dover. Now that the yacht was at rest upon perfectly smooth water he enjoyed a temporary relief from the affliction of nausea and an un- usual stability in his nervous system. As there was no likelihood of a breeze before the return of

daylight, his desire to be left in sole charge met
with instant approval. He took his post at the
tiller a proud man, from whose eye gleamed the
light of adventure and upon whose brow was
graved deep the frown of determination.

That evening off Fairlight the yacht plunged
along crazily with wind ahead and a troublesome
sea. The sky was thought to wear a look of wildness and, as a preparation for possible bad
weather, it was determined to snug the ship
down by striking the topmast. B. B. undertook
the task of removing the fid. Wire shrouds offer
no easy climbing and to unpractised hands and
legs are almost impossible of ascent. With much
puffing and panting the volunteer swarmed
slowly upwards. The impatient mate clambered
to the cross-trees up the hoops of the mainsail,
pulled out the fid and was back on deck again
before B. B. had abandoned the support of the
convenient light-board. Though infinitely relieved to be quit of his task, he protested with
severity that, even if it possessed the merit of
speed, this method of going aloft was both illegiti-
mate and unseamanlike. Unwonted exertion
played havoc with his vacillating stomach. He
refused tea with loathing and retired to his cot.

Instead of bad weather a beautiful night came
with a breeze off the land. Soon after dark when
the yacht was slipping quietly past Hastings, she
ran into a drift-net. Before the skipper at the

"SENORITA," PREPARING FOR A PASSAGE

tiller had fully realized what had happened, B. B. darted up through the hatchway and made as though to fling himself incontinently overboard.

"Hullo! whither away so fast?" ejaculated the startled skipper. "Are you dreaming or sleep-walking or gone off your head?"

"The yacht is ashore!" was B. B.'s astonishing reply.

"Ashore be hanged! She's foul of a net. The shore is a couple of miles to windward."

To quiet his fears he had pointed out to him the floats of the net, the lines of phosphorescence extending from either bow, the safe distance of the dimly visible land and the brilliant lights of Hastings Pier. Hardly could he be satisfied that they were not in dire peril of their lives.

"But I heard her bottom scrape along the pebbles as she ran up the beach!" he muttered as he went below reluctantly to face with indifferent patience the wild chuckling of the mate. "Oh shut up!" he exclaimed with a rueful laugh. "No doubt the sound was caused by the net as the yacht scraped along it, but it was just the noise I should have heard had she landed herself on a heap of shingle." The yacht's head was boxed off and by reaching in under the land the end of the net was found and the obstruction rounded.

With wind light and ahead a whole day was spent in working from Beachy Head to the Owers lightship, a day of much distress to B. B., who found the quick motion by no means to his

16

liking, but his spirits revived when just before dark the Wight disclosed its unmistakable outline. Before the Nab lightship was reached it fell almost calm. In the grey dawn of the following morning the yacht slipped between the forts and an hour later was anchored under the indifferent shelter of Ryde pier.

In the afternoon B. B. insisted upon exploring Ryde and dining at an hotel. As it was the middle of the Cowes week the dining-room was crowded with guests interested in yachts and yacht-racing. Finding his surroundings entirely congenial B. B. seemed to expand with benignity and to cast a mantle of benevolence over his embarrassed companions. No bushel was big enough to hide his light. Not a word of boasting issued from his lips, but his stylish yet severely correct yachting garb, his restrained manner and assured bearing discovered to the least observant the owner of a famous yacht or a noted helmsman.

A couple of days were spent about Southampton Water in watching the racing of the smaller fry in which B. B., as the owner of a small racing boat himself, professed to feel the greatest interest. One evening with the effusiveness generated by a satisfying meal he detailed to delighted listeners the virtues of his boat and the persistent bad luck of his racing in her. If his description were literally true she carried a startling amount of canvas and was the fastest craft afloat on the upper waters of the Thames. But ever untoward accident

"Never likely to forget it! But for that lucky slant at the last moment we should have been swept into the torrent and sent to the bottom."

"Ah, swamped to a certainty!"

B. B.'s head appeared. His face was pale, his eyes dilated. With an unconvincing show of nonchalance he said: "Why go into Weymouth at all? With a fair wind why not push across the bay at once?" His fear of the race was even greater than his fear of a night passage.

"By Jove, old chap," replied the skipper after a moment spent ostensibly in grave consideration, "of course you are right. That's the thing to do without a doubt. Ought to have thought of it myself!"

The skipper maintained an unmoved countenance, but the mate all but gave away the plot by inability to mask his merriment. He fled forward upon an imaginary errand, but from behind the mainsail could be heard extraordinary sounds of suppressed laughter. When B. B. manifested surprise, the skipper saved the situation by whispering: "Don't say anything—but I believe the mate is sick?" Concern and amusement lightened for a moment the gloom of an anxious countenance.

Having frightened B. B. into renouncing the comfort of a harbour, they cheerfully altered course to pass outside the Shambles lightship and to give to the race a fitting berth. The wind blew steadily all night. At midnight the yacht was off the Bill, and by 10 a.m. the following forenoon she was moored in Salcombe harbour. B. B. had not enjoyed the run. He insisted upon sharing the mate's trick at the tiller, and, with eye fixed upon the compass card, querulously called him to attention whenever the needle, owing to the yacht's sheers in a lumpy sea, swung a trifle off the given course. "Oh, she'll come back of herself," the mate retorted, refusing to be stampeded into a misuse of the tiller. His coolness did nothing to allay anxiety. What was the good of a tiller except to keep a ship's head exactly to the required bearing?

"Here, steer the boat yourself if you think you can do better!" at last exclaimed the harassed mate. Quickly finding that, in spite of frantic exertion, the yacht was taking charge, B. B. hastily relinquished the duty thrust upon his unskilled hands. At daylight no land was visible. The wind was cold, and B. B. was very wretched. Shivering and overwrought, he tried to forget in sleep the imaginary dangers that beset the yacht. The Start, soon sighted ahead, brought comfort to his heart, but his equanimity was manifestly far from perfect even after the anchor had been dropped and the canvas stowed.

While after lunch skipper and mate enjoyed a sleep in their respective cots, B. B. quietly packed his bag, and, that done, roused the sleepers with the announcement of his immediate departure. He was sorry to leave, but life on board was too hard for his delicate constitution. Another night, at sea, he shamelessly admitted, would drive him crazy. In vain was it pointed out that the coast now reached was rich in harbours and that the need for night passages was past. B. B. turned deaf ears to persuasion and argument. He had made up his mind to go—and go he would. Yielding at length to obduracy the mate rowed him ashore *en route* for Kingsbridge to take train to London.

The skipper remained on board. He tidied up the cabin, disordered by B. B.'s packing, and was vastly surprised to find himself regretting the unexpected break-up of the company. Now that B. B.'s peculiarities were understood, they produced as much amusement as irritation. Nervousness and nausea are misfortunes to be pitied, not faults to be vituperated.

But his regret proved to be uncalled for. In a couple of hours B. B. was back on board. Either exhilarated by a bottle of cider—a beverage of pleasant flavour and innocent reputation—or won over by further persuasion, he repented of his resolve and decided to continue the cruise. Moreover the nearest station was five miles away, and the wheezy rattletrap that linked Salcombe with the outer world paid more attention to tides than to trains, and had puffed away on its last journey up the river. He brought on board a large selection of fishing lines. "I'm a bit of a fisherman!" he exclaimed with a fine air of self-depreciation. He caught no fish, but he caught himself repeatedly. His companions grew adepts in the work of disentanglement.

By easy stages the yacht was worked to Falmouth. The weather was unusually fine, each night was spent in a different harbour, and B. B. admitted that life on a small yacht could have its pleasant side. Skipper and mate were determined to reach Scilly, but well aware that B. B. would recoil from a passage forth into the broad Atlantic, they, with reprehensible deceit, let it be understood that Penzance was to be the limit of their cruising westward. Cunningly they tickled the imagination of B. B. by dilating upon the beauties of the neighbourhood, by weaving romances about the wonders of Mount St.Michael, by planning a drive in one of the conveyances that ply between Penzance and Land's End, by hinting at a *recherché* dinner at a first-class hotel to celebrate the yacht's turning-point and to cement the good fellowship of her crew.

Consequently it was rather with pleasant anticipation than ill-concealed tremulousness that B. B. assisted in getting the yacht under way for the last lap of the outward voyage. The day was dull and heavy, and under the shelter of the town, when for a few moments the sun burst through the clouds, the atmosphere was oppressively hot. The S.W. wind was light, and only slowly was the yacht worked over a foul tide past the Manacles and Black head. At 2 p.m. with W. running stream she rounded the Lizard. The

wind had backed to S. and blew with fitful gusts.
Gloom settled down heavily and obscured the
land. A heavy sea soon sent B. B. to his cot
gloomy as the weather outside, and vowing by
all his gods to leave the yacht the moment
Penzance was reached.

Skipper and mate were cheerful in spite of
threatening weather. They had feared some
trouble with B. B. if on rounding the Lizard he
discovered that the yacht was not heading for
the promised Penzance. Thanks to the elements,
he remained ignorant of their disgraceful machina-
tion. Sky and water combined to render easy his
unconscious conveyance to Scilly. The land was
hidden in murk, and the sea had laid him low
and unable to inspect the compass.

By the time the Wolf Rock lighthouse was
reached the wind was strong and the sea heavier.
Shortly afterwards the yacht was brought to
the wind and the mainsail reefed, the storm jib
substituted for the working jib, and the topmast
housed. The staysail was left a-weather and the
kettle boiled. B. B. refused with a shudder the
offer of food and contemplated with aversion
his companions' enjoyment of a solid meal. The
yacht lay quietly, but the upward rise and
corresponding fall as she alternately breasted a
billow and sank into a hollow, the angry flap of
the mainsail as she came up to the wind, the
lurch to leeward as her head fell off again, the
thump and rush of water when the crest of a sea

crashed upon the foredeck, the lugubrious moan of the wind through the taut weather rigging, all filled the soul of B. B. with an alarm he scarcely attempted to conceal.

" Shall we soon be there?" he asked.

"You will not see Penzance this night, my son. It's as thick as a hedge and we dare not run away to leeward. It is piping up to blow, too. The open sea is the safest place and there we are going to stay." The skipper's words brought no comfort to B. B. Nausea and panic are bad companions for a dirty night.

Soon after the yacht was put upon her course rain began and hampered still further the restricted outlook. At 10 p.m. she was deemed to be near enough to the islands and laid to to wait for daylight or a clearance in the weather. The lights on St. Agnes and on Round Island remained invisible, and near as shelter was, it was unattainable without their help. Several miserable hours were passed, and at each relief of the watch on deck skipper and mate half seriously debated the question whether the beastliness of the night might not be a divine judgment upon them for their inconsiderate treatment of B. B. Sound sleep, they gladly observed, had relieved him from the oppression of imaginary dangers.

Dawn was near when the rain ceased and the wind broke up the low-lying clouds. Soon lights were visible. The tide had swept the yacht within a mile of the Seven Stones lightship, and as the wind was now N.W. a beat of 6 or 7 miles lay between them and the shelter of the islands. Only slow progress was made against the tide through a heavy sea. But in time smoother water was found under the shelter of St. Mary. The yacht mended her pace, and after a board or two in the sound finished the passage by a short run into the pool. The rattle of the cable as the anchor was tumbled overboard brought B. B. in a hurry from his cot.

"Penzance?" he asked as he gazed doubtfully at Hugh Town.

"No, Scilly!"

"Scilly?—but I thought Penzance——"

"Well, you see, the night was thick and dark, and the yacht lost her way, or, perhaps, she blundered up against the islands by accident or by sheer perversity. We are at Scilly all right, whatever the explanation of the yacht's arrival."

B. B. was sensible enough to accept with good grace an accomplished fact without inquiring too closely into the method of its accomplishment. Though he would certainly have refused to make the passage had his wishes been consulted, he was not ill-pleased to find himself exploring unexpectedly the inherent charms of outlying islands. The days of his stay were days of pleasantness. If ever the disturbing thought intruded of the miles of rolling water that lay between him and the mainland, he allowed not the canker of fear to spoil the enjoyment of the present pleasure.

As he strode along the street of Hugh Town, many
an eye, after an appreciative glance at his distinguished appearance, hastily scanned St. Mary's
Roads in search of the big yacht from which he
must have landed. It was incredible that such a
typical yachtsman belonged to a little craft lying
in the pool.

Attractive as the Scilly Islands are, the list of
their attractions is not unending, and the time
came when all on board were ready to begin the
homeward voyage. At 2 p.m. the yacht passed
through Crow Sound, and with topsail and
spinnaker set ran with a steady W. breeze over a
sea that gleamed and quivered beneath the rays
of a dazzling sun. It was hard to believe that this
sportive and dancing sea was the same mass of
water that a few nights before had hampered
the yacht with vicious blows. The motion was
insufficient to cause B. B. much inconvenience.
Moreover, he was homeward bound!

At midnight the Lizard was passed. All the
early morning and following day the wind was
provokingly light, and in the evening, to escape
the weariness of a calm night in the open, the
yacht was worked on the last of a fluttering air
into Cawsand bay, where the lying is good when
the wind blows from the west. Calm weather
continued, and all next day was spent in drifting
slowly across Bigbury bay. At midnight the yacht
was off Bolt Tail. The tide had just turned to the
eastward and a breeze blew gently off the land.

B. B. was anxious to be entrusted with charge and, as it seemed impossible for him to go wrong, the skipper gave him the course and handed over the tiller. The mate was already below and asleep. The head of the skipper had scarce reached the pillow when B. B., in tones of the deepest disquietude, demanded his immediate presence on deck, for a red light was visible, which he seemed unable to avoid. On reaching the deck the skipper found that the red light shone forth from a steamboat, passing to leeward at the distance of a couple of miles. B. B. had run off the course, and, like a moth with a candle, was using every effort to reach the point of attraction.

Shortly before 3 a.m. the sleepers were awakened by cries of urgent alarm. The mate, first on deck, bade the skipper remain where he was, and returning a minute later to the cabin to garb himself for a spell on deck, almost collapsed with hysterical laughter. "The blessed B. B.," he spluttered, "was after running down a ship of the Queen's navee! Right under our bows I found a torpedo boat, not 50 yards away, whistling frantically. The yacht, off before the wind, was aiming straight at her broadside. The torpedo boat, puzzled by her erratic sheers, evidently did not know whether to go ahead or astern. The yacht is on her course again and the torpedo boat well on the road to Plymouth. I'm thankful she has not chased us to get our name and address. B. B.'s teeth are chattering with excitement and the sooner he is in bed the better for all concerned." From Bolt Tail with a fair tide and a nice breeze abeam the yacht in three hours had barely reached the meridian of Prawle Point. B. B. was unable to give any explanation of the small progress made in circumstances so favourable.

All day the yacht lay becalmed a few miles E. of the Start. Provisions were short and tobacco was finished. A grumpy and short-tempered pair lolled about listlessly sucking empty pipes. When gloom was merging into despair B. B. produced an overlooked tin of tobacco from the depths of his bag. Their sighs of relief brought a momentary quiet to the canvas. With B. B. smoking was rather a pose than a pleasure, and he was unable to enjoy the strong tobacco which he had brought on board as suited to the stout stomachs of seafarers. He seemed to be inexperienced in the use of a pipe, for he held it in his front teeth like a cigar and kept it alight as much by blowing down as by drawing up the stem. His tobacco was therefore smoked without searching of heart or pricking of conscience.

Early the following morning the yacht was discovered to be approaching the Chesil Beach, greatly to the astonishment of the navigators. During the many hours of calm she had been sucked deeply into the bay. The allowance made for indraught had been ludicrously insufficient. There was at the moment a nice N. breeze, and

B. B. was trusted to steer in pursuit of a schooner yacht, evidently eastward bound. At breakfast he declared that he had been sorely tempted to run through the race to see what it was like. His bravado was received with a chuckle. The slight bucketing experienced a few hours later in St. Alban's Race proved very clearly that his new-found courage was based upon a flimsy foundation.

At breakfast all the provisions were finished except a handful of potatoes, a jar of salt, and one biscuit apiece. Consequently, when, within two miles of the Needles, the yacht was held up by a calm, the menace of famine produced irritable tempers. Late in the afternoon a breeze arose from S.W. which soothed irritation and carried them quickly to Totland bay, where the moment the anchor had a hold B. B. was dispatched to the shore to secure a sufficiency of food to stay ravenous appetites.

The next day they had a rapid run to South-ampton, and here so far as B. B. was concerned the cruise came to an end, for letters were found which, owing to illness in his family, demanded him at home. With mixed feelings he collected his belongings, for while no doubt he was de-lighted to be freed from the anxieties that harassed him at sea, no man leaves a yacht upon which he has lived for a month without a sense of regret. Skipper and mate went to the station to carry his luggage and speed his departure. Though he was the possessor of only a humble third-class ticket, the porters treated him with the respect usually reserved for a duke. His bearing and attire bestowed upon him a dignity rarely worn even by real owners of titles.

The mate learnt on his return home that an impression prevailed among his fellow-townsfolk that but for B. B.'s courage and skill in moments of difficulty the yacht would have been lost and her crew sent to the bottom. It transpired that the loss of his bag on the journey home necessitated, or was made an excuse for, the wearing for several days of a cap and clothing that smacked of the sea. These and the way he wore them gave the impression without any words. One old lady was heard to declare that the British were a nation of sailors and that B. B. was her *beau idéal* of a British tar. Dear old thing—had she but known!

This cruise was B. B.'s first and last venture afloat. Instead of selling a farm and going to sea— a proverbial folly in the eyes of sailor men—he sold his boat and became a squire. He was the best of good fellows ashore, but the following lines by an unknown minor poet might well have been composed to meet his case :

> "The queer sort of up and down motion,
> Which one meets on the treacherous ocean,
> Has quite filled my soul with the notion,
> I never was meant for the sea."